INSIDE PEE-WEE'S PLAYHOUSE

INSIDE PEE-WEE'S PLAYHOUSE

The Untold, Unauthorized, and Unpredictable Story of a Pop Phenomenon

CASEEN GAINES

ECW PRESS

Published by ECW Press
2120 Queen Street East, Suite 200, Toronto, Ontario, Canada M4E 1E2
416-694-3348 / info@ecwpress.com

This book is not affiliated with *Pee-Wee's Playhouse*, nor is it endorsed or approved by Paul Reubens.

Library and Archives Canada Cataloguing in Publication

Gaines, Caseen, 1986-
Inside Pee-wee's playhouse : the untold, unauthorized, and unpredictable story of a pop phenomenon / Caseen Gaines.

ISBN 978-1-55022-998-1
also issued as:
978-1-77090-041-7 (PDF); 978-1-77090-040-0 (EPUB)

1. Pee-wee's playhouse (Television program). I. Title.

PN1992.77.P44G35 2011   791.45'72   C2011-902819-0

Developing Editor: Jen Hale
Book Design and Typesetting: Cyanotype
Index: Terecille Basa-Ong
Printing: Courier   1   2   3   4   5

Printed and bound in the United States

ECW PRESS
ecwpress.com

For my brother, Curtis,
As proof you can do anything you put your mind to
and a reminder not to rush to put aside childish things

TABLE OF CONTENTS

INTRODUCTION 1

1 FROM THE GROUNDLINGS UP 7

2 THE PITCH AND THE HIT 35

3 PUPPETLAND, CALIFORNIA 69

4 A CHRISTMAS STORY 101

5 FORECLOSURE 115

6 P2K 125

7 APPRAISING THE PLAYHOUSE 145

8 EPISODE GUIDE 153

AFTERWORD 207

THE PUPPETLAND DIRECTORY 209

ACKNOWLEDGMENTS 215

NOTES 217

INDEX 221

INTRODUCTION

"Quality television programming can open wide the windows of curiosity for children and enable them to share in the wonder of man's experience."

— Ronald Reagan, October 13, 1986

IN THE SPRING of 1986, Saturday morning children's television was popular, profitable, and predictable. The three major television networks, ABC, CBS, and NBC, aired cartoons that lacked in originality and, for the most part, had no educational value. There were superheroes (*Spider-Man and His Amazing Friends*, *The Super Powers Team: Galactic Guardians*), animated adaptations of live-action movies and TV shows (*It's Punky Brewster*, *Star Wars*), new shows with established characters (*Alvin and the Chipmunks*, *The Smurfs*), and even a show starring a larger-than-life wrestling personality (*Hulk Hogan's Rock 'n' Wrestling*).

As children urged their parents to empty their wallets for toys based on their favorite Saturday morning cartoons, some parents began paying closer attention to children's programming, and many didn't like what they saw. Critics described the networks' lineups as being filled with "program-length commercials" for merchandising

© John Duke Kisch / CBS

1

like Pound Puppies, G.I. Joe, and Care Bears. Peggy Charren, the founder and president of Action for Children's Television, claimed that Saturday morning TV was "filled with do-goody nonsense" and she urged networks to introduce shows with more educational value. With the scrutiny of children's television increasing, President Ronald Reagan established National Children's Television Awareness Week that October, a month after the new season of Saturday morning programming debuted. Television as we knew it would be forever changed.

Into the Saturday morning television war zone stepped Pee-wee Herman, the man-child in a too-small gray suit of armor, a soldier of a new era of creative children's programming. While *Pee-wee's Playhouse* was hardly the first show to blend animation, puppetry, and live-action — PBS's *Sesame Street* had crossed that bridge almost 20 years earlier — it added a subversive, hipster sensibility to the format, providing a gust of fresh air to a tired timeslot reserved for the stale ideas of network execs.

Playhouse's impact was immediate. The *Washington Post* described the program as "utterly magical, beautifully realized, and veritably giddy with plaintive charm." The show gained the respect of parent advocacy groups and critics alike for being the lone Saturday morning children's show that was not completely animated. In the weeks following its debut, *Playhouse* was frequently cited as being not only the best new show of the season, but the best program on Saturday morning, period.

As William S. Burroughs once said, "In the magical universe there are no coincidences and there are no accidents." This was certainly true for *Playhouse*. The show not only provided a generation of children with something wildly entertaining to watch as they ate their sugared cereal, but it also became symbolic of a national changing of the guard. Just as cassette players had replaced turntables, the new and inventive consumed the old and traditional. Video killed the radio star. *Pee-wee's Playhouse* killed *The Smurfs*.

In fact, it was the popularization of a new and inventive technology that introduced me to Pee-wee Herman. In 1985, my grandpa purchased his first VCR and began taping everything he was remotely interested in that aired on pay-cable networks. By 1986, the surprise success of the film *Pee-wee's Big Adventure* ensured that it would be placed in heavy rotation on HBO, often coupled with 1981's *The Pee-wee Herman Show* special, which had regained attention as Pee-wee became a household name. My grandpa would sit down with me, before I could even form complete sentences, to watch Pee-wee double features. My parents were aware of my interest and they turned the television to *Pee-wee's Playhouse* on Saturday mornings. I watched religiously, often screaming the secret word at the top of my lungs whenever it flashed on the screen and jumping up and down in my footed pajamas. I owned the pull-string doll, which now sounds more like one of the Chipmunks, and it traveled with me to family gatherings, on long car rides, to birthday parties, and everywhere else my parents would let me carry it. One of my cousins had a few episodes on tape that I begged her to watch with me whenever I went over to visit. There are home movies of me imitating Pee-wee's laugh and obnoxiously asking my family the quintessential rhetorical question, "I know you are, but what am I?"

When I started working on this book, I believed myself to be the biggest Pee-wee fan around. However, during the two years I spent working on this project, I found thousands of fans all over the world who have kept their love for Pee-wee alive. Birgit Schuetze, a fan from Germany, spent close to $3,000 to fly to the States to see Pee-wee Herman on Broadway last year. Perry Shall of Philadelphia has a full-sleeve tattoo of the *Playhouse* characters on his arm, with a large illustration of Jambi the Genie on his chest. Ben Zurawski of Chicago, an artist who makes replicas of *Playhouse* characters, coordinated with the producers of the recent stage show at Club Nokia in Los Angeles to propose to his girlfriend Summer Violett, also a fan, on the *Playhouse* set.

Fans Birgit Schuetze and Kevin Buell at *The Pee-wee Herman Show*

Fans like Birgit, Perry, Ben, and Summer are not alone. There has been overwhelming support for Pee-wee on social networking sites, with over half a million people linked with him on Twitter alone. Thousands of fans have shown up to see Paul Reubens, the man behind Pee-wee's make up, at public appearances throughout the years with requests for him to sign 15-year-old merchandise and say some of Pee-wee's signature lines. These are the fans who caused Cartoon Network's Adult Swim reruns of *Playhouse* to average nearly 1.5 million viewers a night in 2004, and who have defended Reubens throughout his various personal and professional struggles.

Over the last two years I reached out to over 200 people affiliated with the show — including Reubens himself, but I was informed that he was reserving his memories for a future memoir. As I told his manager, when his book comes out, I will be among the first to preorder a copy. Reubens' reflections of creating what *TV Guide* called one of the top 10 cult classics of all time will undoubtedly be worth reading. However, in speaking to others involved in the show's creation, I realized that there are hundreds of other stories that can be told about bringing *Pee-wee's Playhouse* to the screen. What I found most striking during the interviewing process was the pride and affection that everyone I spoke to felt for the show and for their own accomplishments, despite some of their personal feelings about Reubens and problems behind the scenes. Twenty-five years later, many of the show's crew described *Playhouse* as

Perry Shall's ode to the *Playhouse*

the best job they'd ever had. The show's lasting success is due to the contributions of a number of talented individuals, many of whom allowed their stories to be told in these pages.

My goal with this book is to trace how a show that must have sounded bizarre on paper managed to captivate the public's attention throughout the '80s. Every once in a while something comes along that becomes a dominating force in our society, often without reasonable explanation. For five years, *Pee-wee's Playhouse* was it. Off camera, there were personal and professional complications that weighed on the production, yet the end result was often pitch perfect. The exact reasons for the show's success and its lasting impact on our culture are difficult to define, but my hope is that this book will help readers form their own hypotheses.

Playhouse fans Ben Zurawski and Summer Violett, a year after their engagement

This book is for loyal fans of *Pee-wee's Playhouse* who watched every Saturday morning, as well as for those who always secretly wanted to know what the fuss was all about. This book is for parents who have introduced their children to the show, as well as for teenagers who have recently discovered the show on reruns and DVD. This book is for girls who wanted to be Miss Yvonne and boys who substituted their mothers' heels for Pee-wee's platform shoes when dancing along to "Tequila." Most importantly, this book is for the hundreds of people who worked tirelessly behind the scenes to contribute to a pop culture phenomenon and the millions of fans around the world, like myself, who always wanted to take a look inside Pee-wee's playhouse.

Caseen Gaines with Prudence Fenton, animation and effects producer for *Pee-wee's Playhouse*

Caseen Gaines with John Paragon and Lynne Stewart

Caseen Gaines with Phil LaMarr

A promotional still of 17-year-old Paul Rubenfeld in Asolo Repertory Theatre's 1970 production of *Life With Father* alongside Isa Thomas, Robert Britton, and William Pitts.

1 | FROM THE GROUNDLINGS UP

INSIDE PEE-WEE'S PLAYHOUSE in the late night of February 7, 1981, Miss Yvonne, the most beautiful woman in Puppetland, and her boyfriend Kap'n Karl, joined Jambi the Genie in a magic spell to make their pal's wish to fly come true. The trio, along with their friends Hermit Hattie, Mailman Mike, Mr. and Mrs. Jelly Donut, and nearly a hundred onlookers, loudly and methodically repeated the magic words: *mekka lekka hi mekka hiney ho*. With a clap of thunder the lights went out, and from the darkness a nasal voice cried, "I'm flying!" prompting an eruption of laughter and applause from the sold-out audience at the Groundling Theatre in Los Angeles.

"I'm Pee-wee Herman," he said. "I'm the luckiest boy in the world." He flew off into the night sky, waving goodbye to all the adult boys and girls who had just watched the first performance of *The Pee-wee Herman Show*, the live precursor to what would become the most groundbreaking Saturday morning children's program of the 1980s, *Pee-wee's Playhouse*.

Pee-wee Herman, with his wonderland of puppets, vintage educational videos, and classic cartoons, seemed to be plucked out of a 1950s television set. Twenty-five years before *The Pee-wee Herman Show* opened at the Groundling Theatre, Paul Rubenfeld, a young kid from Peekskill, New York, huddled before the living room television set with his brother Luke and sister Abby to watch children's programming like *Howdy Doody* and *Captain Kangaroo*. These shows followed a basic format that was reproduced on a countless number of local television networks across America: a charismatic host speaks directly to the viewing audience, there are simplistic puppets, and crazy friends drop by at random. Decades after those young viewers reached adulthood, many still held fond memories of these programs, including the young boy who had since changed his name and moved to Los Angeles, where he was hoping to catch his big break.

A STAR IS BORN

Pee-wee's imaginative world had its formal unveiling at the Groundling Theatre, the home of an improvisational comedy troupe and an acting school where the relatively unknown Paul Reubens honed his comedic skills. The show was a creative collaboration of Groundling talent, as was the evolution of Pee-wee himself.

Reubens began at the Groundlings as a student in a class taught by Phyllis Katz in 1978. As a culminating project, Katz announced that the class was going to prepare a "scene night," similar to the showcases produced by West Hollywood's The Comedy Store, to be performed in-house for other Groundlings and invited guests. Each student would develop a character and perform a short stand-up act.

For Reubens, this was a dream project. While a student at the California Institute of the

PAUL RUBENFELD

"Paul"

Peekskill, New York

Theatre 70, Pres.
National Thespian Society
Art Club
Advanced Mixed Chorus
Best Actor

© Seth Poppel

Paul Reubens in high school

Arts, he had been encouraged by friend Charlotte McGinnis to appear with her on *The Gong Show*. Before that time, he'd had aspirations of being a dramatic actor in the style of James Dean, but McGinnis's offer intrigued him. He decided to give comedy a try.

Reubens and McGinnis performed as the Hilarious Betty and Eddie and won $500 for their performance. He continued to work with McGinnis, and other friends on *Gong Show* acts, ultimately making over a dozen appearances on the show. Reubens realized he had a natural knack for creating larger-than-life characters, and his success on *The Gong Show* inspired him to pursue comedy full-time.

"Being a part of this duo act and coming up with material for *The Gong Show* then led me into the Groundlings, which was an improvisational group that had a real bent towards writing and character creation," Reubens recalled in a 2004 interview with NPR. "It was pretty early in my career where I realized, 'No one's going to do this for me.' I needed to write and create my own vehicle and material."

Although Reubens excelled at character creation, he had difficulty getting started on Katz's assignment. According to Gary Austin, the founder and artistic director of the Groundlings, Reubens was short on ideas for a character and an act. He told Reubens of an 18-year-old aspiring comedian who used to perform at The Comedy Store, where Austin used to emcee.

"The kid's name was Jeff," Austin says. "And because of his age and liquor laws, he was required to sit in the back of the room until two a.m. before he could perform."

According to Austin, Jeff, who refused to give a last name and insisted on being referred to as "Just Jeff," was an unintentionally memorable performer. He looked like Bobby Kennedy's assassin and his act revolved around a shopping bag filled with props that Just Jeff would crack jokes about. None of the jokes worked.

"He would bring out a transistor radio and announce, 'I will now do my impression of a disc jockey,'" Austin says. "He turned on the radio and moved his lips as if he was lip synching a disc jockey, but he never knew what would actually be playing on the radio at that moment and it was never a disc jockey. It was usually a song or a commercial or a ball game, anything but a speaking DJ. This was the nature of his act."

Austin recounted Just Jeff's characteristics and mannerisms to Reubens, and other class-mates suggested ways to exaggerate his behavior. Reubens began improvising, reinventing Just Jeff's prop routine and speaking in a voice he had created during a 1970 production of *Life with Father* at Sarasota's Asolo Repertory Theatre. Reubens grabbed a bag and some props from around the room. He began playing with his "bag of tricks," laughing his now-classic laugh that seamlessly flowed from his new character. Within moments, Pee-wee Herman — named after a "crazy, high-powered kid" Reubens had known as a child — was born.

Austin remembered a tailored glen plaid suit that had once been in his wardrobe's heavy rotation until his friends derided him for its lack of style. The suit was now reserved exclusively for when Austin was auditioning for nerd roles, so he suggested Reubens borrow it. Reubens agreed sight unseen.

The night of the perfor-mance, Reubens arrived with a white dress shirt and match-ing patent-leather shoes. He borrowed a black bowtie from another classmate and put on Austin's suit. With his costume complete and his routine ready, Pee-wee Herman took the stage for the first time.

Reubens' performance was the standout moment of the showcase, and it led to regular bookings at the venue. For a year, he performed for ten minutes a night, making slight alterations to his routine. He began inviting audience members onto the stage and peppering his act with classic

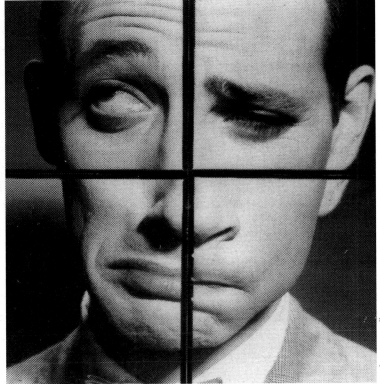

An early version of Pee-wee Herman

schoolyard taunts like "I know you are, but what am I?" and "Why don't you take a picture? It'll last longer!"

"At first he was sort of a bratty kid," Austin remembers. "He was kind of offensive, but he became nicer and more appealing."

Initially, Pee-wee was not the only character in Reubens' arsenal. Among them were Joe Longtoe, a Native American chief with a propensity for dancing on his toes, and Al and Arnie, a pair of corpulent friends whom Reubens created along with fellow Groundling John Paragon.

"There were so many characters," Austin recalls. "I never thought that Pee-wee was his best character. I thought he had better ones. It just turns out that, for whatever reason, that's the one he chose to really pursue, and it made his career."

© The Groundlings

The many faces of Paul Reubens

Reubens' other characters took a backseat as Pee-wee took on a life of his own.

"I used to do this thing [as Pee-wee] where I'd say things like 'Who's got a hard-boiled egg?" Reubens remembered in a 2004 interview with *Los Angeles Magazine*. "I knew something weird was going on when people started coming to shows with that stuff."

As Melrose Avenue began to gain more shops that catered to the new wave and punk scenes, the Groundling Theatre attracted more attention from people in the entertainment industry looking for something new. And in 1980, Reubens caught the eye of three individuals who dramatically altered the course of his career.

WOWING THE AUDIENCE

Doug Draizin went into the Groundling Theatre one night after drinks with friends. He was an agent working for the Agency of Performing Arts (APA), but that night, work was the farthest thing from his mind. He took a seat in the front row and soon found himself engaged in a tête-à-tête with Pee-wee, the character throwing Tootsie Rolls into the audience right at Draizin.

When Draizin returned home, he couldn't shake the memory of his experience and the unique comedian who had engaged him from the stage. He decided to return the following week with two friends.

"We sat there," Draizin recalls, "and after the show they looked at me and said, 'This guy's terrific.' You've got to go back there and talk to him.'"

Despite the advice of his friends, the agent left without speaking to Reubens.

The following day Draizin was walking to his office on Sunset Boulevard and ran into Tracy Newman, a Groundlings member he recognized from his previous trips to the theater. Draizin expressed interest in Reubens and within a few days, Newman had brokered a meeting between the two. Reubens and Draizin hit it off right away, and, at the end of the meeting, the agent offered Reubens representation. All he had to do, he said, was run it by his bosses at APA before things became official.

Despite his excitement about discovering new talent, Draizin's enthusiasm was challenged when he returned to the office.

"I brought his headshot to the agency," Draizin says. "It was an eight by ten with 'Say hello to Pee-wee' written on it. I passed it around the office and told the bosses that I wanted to sign him. They all looked at the headshot and thought it was a joke."

Unbeknownst to his bosses, Draizin signed Reubens anyway.

Shortly after Reubens signed with Draizin, the stoner-comedy duo of Cheech Marin and Tommy Chong made their way to the Groundling Theatre, scouting talent for their latest film.

"I made a few trips down to the Groundling Theatre on Melrose and used talent from there to cast the remaining roles [in *Cheech and Chong's Next Movie*]," Chong explains. "Paul Reubens was our first choice because he was the funniest original talent I had ever seen. His character Pee-wee Herman came to life as a separate entity."

Pee-wee Herman made his film debut in *Next Movie*. At first, the character appears as a wimpy, foul-mouthed hotel clerk who attempts to get the duo arrested. He reemerges later in the film in full performance mode with his trademark look and routine. The film was a commercial success, and many reviewers singled out Pee-wee's sequences as high points.

Pee-wee Herman makes his screen debut in *Cheech and Chong's Next Movie*

Even comedian Steve Martin took note of Reubens' performance. Martin, who was signed to APA, went into a meeting at his agency to lobby for Reubens to be signed.

"He came in and said, 'There's a guy named Paul Reubens, a.k.a. Pee-wee Herman,'" Draizin recalls. "My bosses just looked at me. I said, 'Yeah, he's great. We represent him.'"

With the attention Pee-wee was attracting on stage and screen, Draizin began submitting the character's headshot to casting agents around the country. Within no time, the casting directors at *Saturday Night Live* wanted to "say hello to Pee-wee." Reubens auditioned and made it to the final round of callbacks, but lost the job to Gilbert Gottfried. For Reubens, *SNL* was the holy grail of opportunities. Rejected, he flew back to Los Angeles to regain his spot tossing Tootsie Rolls in the Groundling Theatre.

ANSWERING THE DOOR

Opportunity came in the form of Dawna Kaufmann, a television producer with an idea and a problem. She was the associate producer on a short-lived CBS late-night comedy show called *No Holds Barred*, a program designed to compete directly with *SNL* by featuring a similar style of humor. However, censors frequently accused the show of presenting content that was inappropriate for network television, so frequently in fact that every episode was a struggle to get on the air. The torturous process inspired Kaufmann to come up with ideas for television show concepts that would be immune from the censors' knives.

Dawna Kaufmann

"If you want to be edgy, you've got be a little clever," she explains. "So I thought it would be wise to come up with a late-night show that couldn't be touched by the censors because we would never say a naughty word and we would never have any explicit sexuality. We wouldn't have anything we could be attacked for, but it would be subversive. Everyone would know what we were talking about, but we wouldn't be directly saying anything that would put us at risk."

She thought about other kinds of shows that had a similar format. As her brain raced through all of the flickering images she had seen on television, she thought of a novel question — what if television's future lay in its past?

"Variety shows always resonated with me," Kaufmann recalls. "I remembered watching Soupy Sales when I was a kid. He'd literally open a door and something exciting would happen. As a little kid I watched lots of those shows and I was deeply influenced by them and that style of entertainment. That was the motivation to come up with a show that had a playhouse idea. It would have a narrative structure, but every couple of minutes something would happen. A new door would open and you'd be taken on a new ride, sometimes with puppets or cartoons, but it would always be different."

Kaufmann told her best friend, actress Cassandra Peterson (who later went on to pop-notoriety as the cult icon Elvira, Mistress of the Dark), about her late-night television show idea. A light bulb switched on over Peterson's head.

"She was in the Groundlings and told me there may be someone in the group that would have ideas I could work with to create a show," Kaufmann recalls. "I had contacts in the industry and could pitch the show to plenty of people in show business. So I went down and saw Paul's act and thought, 'Well, here's a guy who would make a good host.'"

Peterson took the producer backstage after the show and introduced her to Reubens.

"I wanted to do a show for television; didn't have much money, but had a lot of contacts," Kaufmann recalls. "He mentioned he had an agent and contacts too. We decided to put our heads together and start working on a show."

Kaufmann and Reubens went out to dinner the following day to discuss the particulars of *The Pee-wee Herman Show*, their new venture titled after *The Pinky Lee Show* and *The Soupy Sales Show*. With their sights set on television, Kaufmann decided to market the stage show as a "live pilot" for network television consideration and provide as many industry insiders as possible with comp tickets in the hopes that one of them would offer a deal. Because of his access to actors, Reubens would spearhead casting. In turn, Kaufmann would be responsible for recruiting the crew. However, even if they didn't pay cast and crew, there would be costs associated with producing a live television pilot. They'd need to construct sets, print posters, and mail hundreds of promotional materials publicizing the event. Although both partners wanted to give this their all, neither had the money to make it happen. Reubens excused himself from the table and made a telephone call to his parents Judy and Milton Rubenfeld, asking them for a loan of $8,000. They agreed.

"The first time we made money on the show a check got cut to them," Kaufmann recalls. "It was really helpful for Paul to ask Milton and Judy for the money. It gave us the ability to make the show a reality."

According to Doug Draizin, Reubens had been interested in expanding his presence at the Groundlings to a full-length performance even prior to Kaufmann's offer.

"Paul and I had discussed doing a one-man show at the Groundlings, with him doing different characters," Draizin recalls. "But the Groundlings weren't having it. They thought it was a conflict of interest. There was a lot of politics."

The first person brought on to the proposed TV show was Groundling Phil Hartman, whose improvisational skills proved crucial in providing a much-needed boost of confidence for Kaufmann and Reubens. During their first meeting together, Hartman created the character of Kap'n Karl; it was so perfect, the young producer knew immediately that the show had the potential of landing a network television deal.

"You know when you've got it right and I knew we had it the minute Phil sang the hand-washing song during our first meeting," she recalls. "It was so hilarious and Paul's reaction to it was right on."

Fellow Groundlings Edie McClurg, John Moody, John Paragon, and Lynne Stewart were among the first cast. Reubens asked them to come up with original characters that would fit the show's avant-garde format, and within no time, iconic characters like Jambi the Genie, the disembodied, green head-in-a-box; Kap'n Karl, the salty seaman with caterpillar-like eyebrows (named after Kaufmann's father); and Miss Yvonne, the buxom beauty with a bouffant, were born.

In creating her character, Lynne Stewart fashioned

Phil Hartman

Miss Yvonne's dainty yet feisty demeanor after Sandra Dee and Marilyn Monroe. Creating a character and having the ability to run with ideas creatively is Stewart's strong suit.

Lynne Stewart

"Lynne is one of the best comedy character actors in this country in terms of women who create their own characters as opposed to women who play ones that a playwright created," Gary Austin says. "She creates incredibly great comedy characters. Some of the best characters I've ever seen have come from Lynne Stewart."

In addition to the humans, the appropriately named Puppetland was inhabited by a handful of characters made of cloth and foam. Phil Hartman voiced Monsieur LeCroq, an ornery reptilian wingman for his business partner, Mailman Mike, while Edie McClurg created Clocky, a large papier-mâché yellow-and-red map of the United States that would remind Pee-wee of his appointments. John Paragon voiced one of the most integral puppet characters, Pterry-Dactyl, Kap'n Karl's pet. A rod held up the main frame of Pterry-Dactyl's body and controlled his mouth movement, while two more manipulated his wings. Although his appearance would later change, his frame was thin with a bright red tongue permanently hanging out of his mouth and thick brown eyebrows to match his seafaring owner.

For many of the Groundlings, the opportunity to work on a live project that would hopefully give way to a television deal was a dream come true. While several Groundlings were included in the show, there were even more who hoped to be included in the production in the future.

"They kept saying they were going to add more parts for people," Groundling Joan Leizman recalls. "Nobody really knew if it was going to happen."

Cassandra Peterson wouldn't have minded a chance to share the stage with her peers.

"In the Groundlings, I always did these sex-symbol characters, so Paul didn't really see a place for me in the show," she recalls. Instead, Peterson worked as an usherette, handing out programs, while dressed as a little girl in a yellow-and-white gingham dress.

Paul Reubens and Lynne Stewart in rehearsals

Brian Seff and Monica Ganas as Rick and Ruby

In addition to casting Groundlings, Reubens recruited the musical comedy duo Rick and Ruby, played by Brian Seff and Monica Ganas. He had first heard of them after a member of the Groundlings saw them play in 1978 at Robin Williams' wedding in San Francisco. She told Reubens that if the band ever played a gig in Los Angeles, he would have to go see them. When the band played The Palomino Club in North Hollywood in 1979, Reubens attended with gifts in hand.

"There were these three toy ray guns in our dressing room when we were finished with our set, with a note that read 'a gift from a fan,'" Brian Seff recalls. "They were from Paul. He came backstage and invited us to see his act at the Groundling."

Ganas and Seff went to see him and loved the act. The three maintained a long-distance friendship for the following year until Reubens called with an invitation for Rick and Ruby to appear as Mr. and Mrs. Jelly Donut in his upcoming show. They agreed and relocated to L.A.

Two additional non-Groundlings were involved with the show. Mario "Ivan" Flores, a Mexican teenager who lived near the theater, was cast in the small part of Salvador Sanchez. Dora Romani, a singer in her seventies, performed an opening number before performances.

"She was a woman that Paul and I knew from a little Italian restaurant," Kaufmann recalls. "Dora was about five feet tall and five feet wide, a little butterball grandma. She was an opera singer and loud like Ethel Merman, shamelessly going from man to man and heaving her bosoms in their faces. She would sing to them and push their girlfriends out of the way while she sat on their laps. It was hilarious."

As Reubens was assembling an acting army, Kaufmann created a crew. Although underground artist Gary Panter is best known for his illustrations, Kaufmann knew him from a punk manifesto he wrote in the early 1970s. She invited him to see Reubens perform at the Groundling and asked him to contribute to the show. Panter liked the act and suggested he serve as production designer; his responsibilities would eventually include publicity illustrations, set design, and puppet fabrication.

With Gary Panter came his wife, Nicole, a musician with a large local following due, in part, to her time managing the underground punk band The Germs. She was brought on as "the cool consultant," appraising the scripts to find bits that worked and those that didn't.

Upon Gary's recommendation, Kaufmann hired Jay Cotton to compose and play the show's score. Although Cotton's behavior was often wild and unpredictable during

Gary Panter holding the soundtrack for *The Pee-wee Herman Show* that features his artwork

rehearsals, his musical abilities exceeded everyone's expectations.

"The little flourishes Jay put in were so creative," Kaufmann recalls. "They were like exclamation points at the end of every song. They were thrilling to listen to."

"Jay's very talented," Nicole Panter explains. "He's crazy as a shithouse rat, but in him Paul got someone very talented who was willing to work for very, very cheap."

Guy Pohlman, a member of the show's technical crew and Cotton's understudy, agrees with Nicole's sentiments about his talents.

"He was a fair pianist, but he had a vision for that show," Pohlman recalls. "He had a sense of humor and it fit perfectly with the Groundlings. He had the tone exactly right for a children's show that was a little risqué."

The cast collaborated on the script, drawing on their unique talents and senses of humor to produce the live pilot.

"The show was initially created by Dawna with Paul, but once that snowball started rolling down the hill, the rest of us were incorporated into it and added our body of knowledge and cultural references to it," Nicole Panter explains. "Phil Hartman and Edie McClurg both contributed elements to the show that are beyond value. They were very similar in that they had a very deep well of material to draw from. Both of them were really well-spoken, quick-on-their-feet performers. I see their fingerprints all over the show."

By day, Kaufmann would audio record the improvisational rehearsal and turn them into script pages at night. She remembers the writing process fondly.

"I loved collaborating with everyone and I think Paul did too," Kaufmann recalls. "We'd go out to dinner usually and talk about what worked and what didn't work. Then I would go home and I would write a new script, and the next night at rehearsal we'd go through it, and if people had new ideas to add, we'd throw them in."

Paul Reubens and Phil Hartman rehearse, and Pee-wee Herman and Hermit Hattie (Edie McClurg) on stage

While developing the script, the Pee-wee Herman character began to grow as well. As unlikely as it might have seemed when the project began, in the months preceding the show's debut, Pee-wee matured. It was like a show had been based around a character from a television commercial.

"When we started, he was not a host of any kind, he was just a character," Kaufmann recalls. "So we all helped [Paul] find his motivation as a character, along with the story line about him wanting to fly. It was exciting to be a part of that and to see it come together. During those days, I really felt I was in Judy Garland and Mickey Rooney world, putting on a show in a garage. We really pulled it off quite nicely."

LIVE FROM LOS ANGELES, IT'S SATURDAY NIGHT

Some of the cast and crew of *The Pee-wee Herman Show*

Reubens arranged for the show to run on midnights at the Groundling Theatre after the Friday and Saturday night regular Groundlings performances, where Pee-wee Herman had made his debut a few years earlier. The cast and crew of nearly 40 worked together to bring the show to fruition as opening night neared.

"Gary created this great lime-green-and-purple poster," Kaufmann recalls. "As we were gearing up to opening, I would go around at night with different people in the cast and we would slap up these posters all over town. I'm amazed we didn't get arrested because that was never a legal thing to do, but it was helping to set the stage for this underground event that was going to be opening."

Kaufmann exhausted her Rolodex to get every person she knew with ties to the entertainment industry in to see the show. While much has been written about the show's runaway success with the public in its early days, most of the audience was made up of Hollywood insiders, not members of the general public.

"I was bringing in everyone who had even a tangential contact in Hollywood," she recalls. "They would all get free tickets. We were just papering the house to get warm bodies in there and build a buzz. It wasn't about making money as a play, it was about getting seen by people who might take interest and want to develop it as a television show."

Steve Martin, Martin Scorsese, Robert De Niro, Robin Williams, Penny Marshall, Regis Philbin, George Carlin, and Lily Tomlin were a few of the "warm bodies" that packed the house at the Groundling Theatre to see the show in its opening weeks.

"At first, it was purely industry," Pohlman recalls. "It was a showcase and nobody was really attracted to it. It was kind of a hidden thing. The mainstream public didn't know anything about it. I took lots of people to the

show and some of them hated it. They just didn't know what to make of the show."

Before working on *The Pee-wee Herman Show*, Guy Pohlman was a student at California State University, Northridge, and he went to see the show after reading a review in the *Herald Examiner*. He recognized Pee-wee Herman from a television appearance the character had made and wanted to experience the comedian live.

"It was always sold out, but if you waited around and someone didn't show up, you might be able to get in," he recalls. "So I waited with about six or seven people ahead of me in line and I got in and loved the show. I kept going back."

After one of his repeated viewings, Pohlman struck up a conversation with Kaufmann about his interest and experience in puppeteering. His enthusiasm convinced her to offer him a job on the technical crew. Pohlman's experience was not unique; many minor cast and crew changes occurred during the show's run.

While the run at the Groundling Theatre was successful, it came with its problems. Kaufmann and Reubens wanted to let in more of the public so that excitement would continue to build. Additionally, the set had to be dismantled after every performance to accommodate the regularly scheduled Groundlings programming that took place during the week. As a result, the decision was made to move the show to The Roxy Theatre on the Sunset Strip, where just a few years earlier, *The Rocky Horror Show* had made its American debut and become a cult classic.

"The Groundlings had a smaller stage. It was harder to fit things on," Pohlman recalls. "The Roxy has a bigger stage and you could light it better. We had a more professional-looking production."

While the bulk of the show was the same, some changes were made before its Roxy debut.

© Ronn Spencer

Pee-wee Herman poses for publicity photos with Joan Leizman, Lynne Stewart, and Nicole Panter

© Abe Perlstein

Pee-wee shares the stage with Kap'n Karl, Miss Yvonne, Dr. Mondo, and Joan Leizman

Nicole Panter joined the cast as Susan, a next-door neighbor who falls victim to Pee-wee's shoe mirrors, and Tito Larriva, another musician from L.A.'s punk scene, played Hammy, her nebbishly perverted brother. And a new segment was created to incorporate Groundling Joan Leizman as an audience member who is hypnotized and convinced to undress by a puppet named Dr. Mondo.

"People really thought I was an audience member," Leizman recalls. "Paul didn't want my name in promotional material because he didn't want people to know I was an actress. I have to admit, when I saw myself on tape I did really look spaced out."

Before joining as a full-fledged cast member, Leizman acted as an understudy for all the female characters in the show. Although cast members rarely missed performances, on the last performance at the Groundling Theatre, Lynne Stewart was a no-show.

"I was about to go home and someone told me to stay and wait," Leizman recalls. "I was asked if I thought I could fill in for Miss Yvonne, and I said sure."

The show was pushed back a half hour to give the actress more time to run lines. Within what felt like no time, the very nervous Leizman prepared to take the stage for her *Pee-wee* debut.

"They made an announcement before the show that an understudy would be playing one of the parts, but they didn't mention my name or which part would be understudied," Leizman recalls. "The performance went pretty well so the audience probably didn't even know which part was being filled in."

Stewart arrived at the theater moments before the show was over.

"At first Paul was a little suspicious," Leizman recalls. "He thought [Lynne and I] had arranged it so I would have a chance to go on, but once he heard that she was upset because her boyfriend's dog had been put down that afternoon, he backed down."

While Reubens and Stewart have maintained a genuinely strong relationship since the start, there were other disputes between Reubens and the cast and crew behind the scenes of *The Pee-wee Herman Show.*

Although their creation was proving successful with Hollywood heavyweights, Reubens and Kaufmann disagreed over whether the show should be opened up to celebrity special guests. Kaufmann had envisioned the show as being slightly unpolished, with the actors free to improvise lines and make the show slightly different from night to night, but Reubens disagreed with this idea, wanting to ensure that there were no surprises on stage that may draw the audience's focus away from the Pee-wee–centered plot.

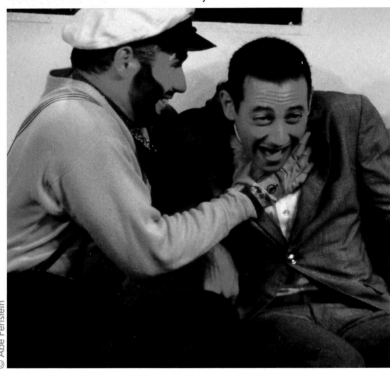

"I always wanted to have someone knock at the door, have Pee-wee answer it and not know who it would be," Kaufmann recalls. "I could have arranged for Steve Martin to walk out or Burt Reynolds. I thought it would be a hoot to have different people popping up and doing a little improv, but he always vetoed that. He didn't want anything that wasn't scripted."

In addition to these arguments over the basic format of the show, there were occasional altercations between Reubens and John Paragon.

"John was a really talented performer who could do somersaults from standing still," Kaufmann remembers. "He was an excellent dancer and could create songs out of thin air. He had an excellent singing voice. His only issue was that he had really bad skin. So what does Paul do? Put John in a role where only his face is visible."

Nicole Panter concurs. "It's really interesting that John Paragon was put in a box," she says. "He was an incredibly physical performer and if he wasn't confined to a box, he might well have stolen the show away from Paul. "

While Kaufmann and Panter believe that Reubens sought to outshine Paragon, Monica

Ganas remembers sharing the stage with Reubens as a positive experience, where his talent and creativity allowed her to shine even brighter. "The first time I interacted with him on stage was a really strong moment. It was really terrific to not be the strongest person on stage and to really concentrate and create. You really had to rise to his level."

GOING THROUGH CHANGES

As the show moved to The Roxy and attracted more public attention, the cast and crew began getting paid $25 per performance. However, for most of them, the money was irrelevant. They had been promised since day one that *The Pee-wee Herman Show* ever made good money, they would all be taken care of.

"We all trusted Paul," Nicole Panter says. "We were all supposed to get a piece of that show."

After opening at The Roxy to huge success, Reubens began consulting with Kaufmann less and with his agents more. APA brokered a deal in which HBO came in and videotaped a performance, to be broadcast as part of its *On Location* comedy series. Kaufmann was less than enthusiastic about the news.

Paul Reubens with his assistant Leslie Williams

"I was not involved in those meetings," she explains. "I think we could have run it as a stage show for another year and built up an even bigger frenzy. We [had only been] doing the show for six months. That's not a very long time when you're just working weekends. I think there was a real hastiness to just sell it to the first interested person."

According to Nicole Panter, the cast was less than enthusiastic about the news as well.

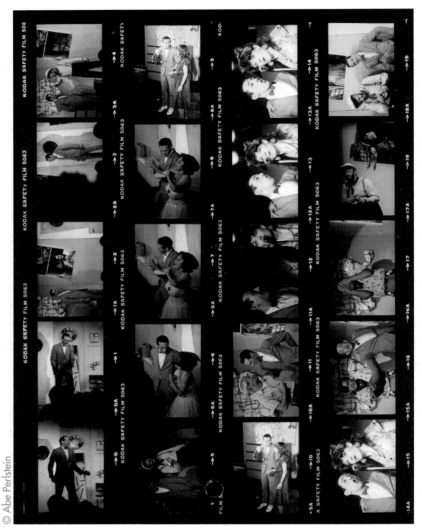

© Abe Perlstein

"You have to remember, to do an HBO show in 1981 was not to be in the company of *The Sopranos*," she explains. "We thought we were going to get a network deal for an ongoing show and all we managed to get was this one-off that was going to sink like a stone because they'd run it for a week and then nobody would see it. It was a consolation prize, but most of us figured it was better than nothing."

Backstage, the mood began changing as the cast and crew felt the show's momentum shift away from its relaxed origins.

"I knew that it was starting to get more serious," Pohlman recalls. "We were really getting into work mode, like a professional sports team headed into the finals. There were bigger people coming in and it felt like things were actually picking up."

Monica Ganas remembers feeling particularly anxious before the HBO taping. "It was so odd because we were in the same venue, but all of a sudden there were lots of cameras," she recalls. "It had a different feel. I remember the producers all looking very stern and I kept thinking, 'My God, I hope I don't do anything to get in trouble.'"

Although the show was gaining momentum, it was decided that *The Pee-wee Herman Show* would end its run the night HBO came to film the show. The show's income was barely enough to cover the cost of paying the cast, crew, and venue. Most importantly, Kaufmann and Reubens, who once started the show with enthusiasm, were falling out of professional love with each other. With the show's run coming to a close, the cast and crew pressed Reubens for the long-delayed written agreements promising that they would remain a team.

"There kept being excuses why the contracts didn't come down, which I now know is an old trick," Nicole Panter explains. "On the eve of filming we were given contracts that were different from what Paul told each of us we would be getting and we were told to sign or tough shit. We all signed, including Dawna, including me, including Gary. It was done in a very underhanded, but standard, show-business way."

The cast members were all paid nominal royalties for their writing credits, because the pie had to be split so many ways, and they were given no additional compensation for their acting work. Kaufmann, who had originally approached Reubens about the concept — her concept — was hit even harder. She received a one-time fee as a producer and was barred from receiving any future money from Pee-wee Herman properties. The deed to Pee-wee's playhouse was officially transferred to Reubens.

"What they did to me was nothing in comparison," Nicole Panter recalls. "What they did to her was unspeakable. She was a cocreator. The entire kiddie-show-for-adults concept was her idea. Before he met her, [Paul] was doing a five-minute routine between scene changes at the Groundlings. It's tragic what they've done to her. And I don't think it would have been as easy to do if she wasn't a woman, and a nice woman at that."

Some would beg to differ with Panter's opinion. For others who worked on the show, the success of *The Pee-wee Herman Show* had more to do with Reubens than the playhouse concept. Guy Pohlman remembers the way Reubens would get everyone excited before going onstage. "There was a huddle right before every show. Everyone would put their hands in and Paul would get into this thing where he would give a little pep talk and we would scream at the tops of our lungs. We were all so excited about the show."

According to Pohlman, most of the cast saw Paul as the leader of their group and the show's driving force. "Paul was the lead man," Pohlman says. "He was in charge. It was his character, his show. The title was *The Pee-wee Herman Show*. It was his baby. There was even a Star of David on his dressing room door at the Roxy as kind of a funny thing. Because he was the star, people would adorn it with things. That door was our way of saying that he was the boss."

Although the process of bringing *The Pee-wee Herman Show* began as a fun ride for many involved, several people still harbor misgivings about the emergency brake being pulled before the ride was at a complete stop.

"For me, the first part of the Pee-wee thing was incredibly fun; to be on stage in Los Angeles in a show during the early eighties that everyone famous wanted to come to was a blast," Nicole Panter recalls. "For that, I'm grateful. But it ended really badly for me and a lot of people."

Pohlman considers the psychology to be fairly common in show business. "When things are starting out, you need people and you're generous. The excitement is genuine and you're kind," he says. "And then when you start to see a path to success, that's when you start to alter yourself. Whoever is in power starts to change the dynamic of their relationships according to their needs. It's like when you're trying to get someone to work on an independent film. In the beginning, it's 'It'll be great, why don't you help out, it'll be a lot of fun.' And then when it makes money, it's 'Well, there was never a contract, but at least you can say you worked on it.'"

For Dawna Kaufmann, whom the *Hollywood Reporter* described as the "mastermind" behind the production in their announcement of the show, it was particularly difficult to see everyone cast aside.

"It made me humiliated and depressed that I couldn't make good on the promises that Paul and I made to the artists that came in to be puppeteers and crew members on the show," she admits. "This really was a family and we were all supposed to get to the next step together. Instead, the kids saw their parents get divorced and they were left to fend for themselves."

While she has never achieved notoriety for her contributions, Kaufmann was instrumental in creating what went on to be a pop culture phenomenon. As Reubens wrote to her in 1981, "to say *The Pee-wee Herman Show* wouldn't exist without [her] would have been the understatement of the year."

"One thing that Dawna indisputably is, which is essential for a producer to be, is that she's a fabulous cheerleader, especially when [people] look weak in spirits," says Nicole Panter. "There were times when it was 'Oh my God, how are we going to do this?' and she was up there on the deck of the *Titanic* saying, 'We can do this.' It was her baby, and it was taken away from her, and not for any reason; she was swimming with sharks and didn't know it."

In the years following *The Pee-wee Herman Show*'s run, Reubens has stated that he alone came up with the idea for a live show on the plane ride home from his *SNL* audition, and that he called his parents from Los Angeles International Airport to ask them to wire him money.

"Dawna's a very good friend and Paul's a very good friend, and I know there's a lot of animosity between them," Cassandra Peterson explains. "It's made it very difficult over the years, because I love them both."

"I've thought about why I haven't sued him in retrospect," Kaufmann muses. "But I loved John Paragon. I loved Lynne Stewart. I just adored them. I wouldn't have wanted to put them on the stand, especially knowing that they're intrinsically tied to Paul economically. He might call them up twenty years later, as he has, and offer them work. Had I put them on the stand to talk about the inception of the show and what my contributions were, I don't think they would have lied, but I think they wouldn't have been as forthright as they could have been."

STARTING AN ADVENTURE

When *The Pee-wee Herman Show* wrapped, Reubens' star appeared to be on the rise. The remainder of the cast and crew went their separate ways while Reubens worked to turn the buzz about his show into a movie deal. Thanks to Marty Klein, Reubens' other agent who worked with Doug Draizin at APA, the actor took regular bookings on *Late Night with David Letterman*. Sometimes he would be interviewed by the host, who would play the straight man for Pee-wee's antics, and sometimes he was simply a featured guest comic.

With Pee-wee a regular presence on national television, his agents landed him a development deal at Paramount Pictures for a feature film. Despite the team's optimism that a film would get the green-light, the script they presented, which Reubens cowrote with Gary Panter, failed to excite the studio. Paramount rejected the script, and that ended any hope that the studio would produce Pee-wee's first feature.

Pee-wee on the set of *Pee-wee's Lemonade Stand,* an unreleased short film from 1983

In the winter of 1983, while Reubens was continuing his regular stints on *David Letterman*, Bill McEuen and Richard Abramson, two film producers who worked with Steve Martin and ran a marketing company, found themselves snowed in in Denver, Colorado. They were there for an advanced screening of Martin's *The Man with Two Brains*. To take their minds off their missed flight home, they turned on the television and saw Pee-wee playing with toys in front of a stone-faced Letterman while the audience laughed excitedly. The two found themselves transfixed by the sight.

According to Abramson, when they returned to Los Angeles, McEuen was still extolling the virtues of the comedian they had seen on *David Letterman*. He discovered the booking was made through APA and called Marty Klein to request a meeting with the actor and offer his services as a manager. Although Klein was willing to broker a sit-down between the two parties, he offered a word of warning.

Abramson remembers the strange advice his friend got: "Marty said Paul's a talented guy, but he's difficult to work with. If you want to give it a try, go ahead."

Reubens agreed to sign on with McEuen as manager. He also left APA for Abramson, a partner of McEuen's. Together, the new team crafted a plan to get the actor a feature film deal.

"We laid out a program like we were marketing a film and set out to market this character," Abramson explains. "The idea was to take him on the road, get a development deal with a studio, make a film, and then do a television series. Most of the time, even the best-laid plans don't happen, but this time, things went completely according to plan."

After a failed attempt to land a development deal with Universal Pictures, McEuen reached out to Robert Shapiro, the former president of theatrical film production at Warner Brothers who had recently resigned to become an independent producer. McEuen pitched him the idea of a Pee-wee feature, and the idea was appealing enough that it prompted Shapiro to sign on as executive producer and campaign to get the project under development at Warner Brothers.

The studio was willing to offer a development deal on a Pee-wee feature, but they expressed concerns about Reubens' limited fan base and presence in the national mainstream. His appearances on *David Letterman* were frequent and grabbed attention, but there were deep concerns about his nationwide popularity and whether people would pay to watch Pee-wee Herman's antics for longer than a few minutes.

Reubens worked on a script with Michael Varhol (a screenwriter and friend of McEuen) and Phil Hartman during the weekdays. On weekends, he embarked on a cross-country, 22-city tour billed as *The Pee-wee Herman Party*. The series of dates, which included a stop at

Carnegie Hall, sold out every performance and generated an abundance of positive publicity in every city Pee-wee played. Abramson invited the executives at Warner Brothers to the final performance, which was held at the Universal Amphitheater in Los Angeles. As expected, the crowd laughed for and cheered as Pee-wee performed for over an hour. Backstage, the executives were handed the first draft of a film script entitled *Pee-wee's Big Adventure*. They skimmed through the first few pages and immediately green-lit the film.

Warner approved a $4 million budget, a small price tag for a feature length movie released by a major studio. According to Abramson, they had approved a director for the film, but it was a choice that neither he, nor McEuen, nor Reubens felt was appropriate for the project. They asked the executives for a week to find another director, one who might be available, acceptable to everyone, and affordable.

"Lisa Henson, Jim Henson's daughter who was an executive at Warner Brothers, suggested we go see *Frankenweenie*, a short film by a new director named Tim Burton," Abramson says. "They were screening it at Fox, but when I got there, it was sold out. A few days later, I was still bothered by missing the screening, so I called up Disney. They set up a screening room for Paul and I and about ten minutes in, we looked at each other and knew this was the guy. We went back to the studio and, within a few hours, Tim was in our offices working on the movie."

Pee-wee outside the women's room during an appearance at Caroline's Comedy Club in New York

© Wendy Basile

Long before Burton rose to fame with films like *Batman*, *Beetlejuice*, and *Edward Scissorhands*, he was a 28-year-old employee of Disney Studios making short films that were rarely seen by anyone outside of the filmmaking crowd. *Frankenweenie* was a short film and it starred Reubens' friend Shelley Duvall, who also felt strongly that Burton would be the right director for *Big Adventure*. With the studio's go-ahead, the newly completed team began working on the film.

"There were a lot of changes made to the script while it was in development and even more when Tim came on board," Abramson says. "Tim had more influence on the film's look and the characters surrounding Paul than [on] the way Paul performed as Pee-wee Herman. I think he left Pee-wee alone because he was smart enough to realize Paul understood the character better than he did."

While Burton mostly took his cues from Reubens when it came to the way Pee-wee would react in certain situations, he did find places in the script where his creativity could fly.

"He added the clown stuff," Abramson recalls. "Actually, we had to cut it back a bit because it was getting too dark. If you look at everything Tim has done, *Big Adventure* is the brightest film he's directed."

For the most part, the collaboration between Burton and Reubens was smooth sailing. Burton was excited to be directing his first feature film, while *Big Adventure* seemed to signal that Reubens may be headed for the stardom he had been working toward.

"Paul had opinions about stuff," Abramson admits, "but [he] fell in love with Tim as a director. They had disagreements about some things, but they were all resolved. He had a lot of faith and trust in Tim."

One of the biggest arguments between Burton and Reubens was over a scene early on in the film where Pee-wee and Francis Buxton, the film's antagonist, engage in a series of schoolyard taunts. According to Abramson, Burton felt the scene was becoming repetitive and monotonous and needed shortening, while Reubens wanted it extended beyond what was written in the script. Ultimately the studio forced a compromise and cut the scene somewhere between where the two parties wanted.

While Burton and Reubens got along well on the set, problems soon arose between the director and the studio. Burton was running the film over budget (in fact, its final cost was just over $6 million) and he was behind schedule, which caused occasional tension on the set.

"Once you start making a film, there isn't much a studio can do besides yell at you for going over budget," Abramson explains. "It was Tim's first live-action feature and it just took longer than we expected for him to shoot it."

Although the film's creative team was excited about *Big Adventure* when production wrapped, Warner Brothers weren't sure they would release it. The studio executives were doubtful that the film would attract an audience and some thought it might be better to cut their losses instead of spending the money making prints of the film and publicizing it across the nation. Reubens and his team were crushed.

"Warner Brothers didn't believe in the picture until it was a total success," Abramson says. "It came out August 9 and, even today, any movie that comes out that late in the summer isn't a film that they plan on running for a long period of time."

The film's producers talked the studio into giving *Big Adventure* a trial run in three cities, and Reubens' team was allowed to choose one of the test screening locations. Abramson and McEuen chose Austin, Texas, a city that had had a particularly strong outpouring of support among college students during the *Pee-wee Herman Party* tour a year earlier. To ensure that Pee-wee's fans turned out to support the film, Abramson came up with a plan.

"I took my own money and made up a little television commercial of still pictures from the movie," he remembers. "We also leaked to the press that Pee-wee was going to make an appearance. We had to turn people away from the movie theater."

Eighty-seven percent of the audience at the Austin test screening stated that they would "highly recommend" the film to others, which was music to the studio's ears. With the other screenings also going well, Warner Brothers scheduled *Pee-wee's Big Adventure* for release and began booking appearances for the character across the nation. Pee-wee Herman, the underground cult star, was entering the mainstream.

2 | THE PITCH AND THE HIT

Michael Chase Walker, the west coast director of children's programming for CBS, was hired by the network to breathe some life into their Saturday morning lineup. While the network was dominating in the primetime ratings thanks to shows like *Murder, She Wrote* and *Dallas*, they were having an impossible time attracting a young audience. Because the network's top-rated shows were attracting viewers over 50 years old, it made little sense to advertise the Saturday morning lineup during their highly successful primetime slot. As a result, the shows the network aired on Saturday mornings got little attention, and CBS consistently finished behind NBC and ABC in the ratings.

Walker's assignment was to acquire new properties that he thought would raise CBS above the pack. With the arguable exception of Jim Henson's *Muppet Babies*, the network was struggling to attract visionaries whose work would appeal to the 6-to-11-year-old age group coveted by Saturday morning advertisers. Walker's background in animation and enthusiasm for the medium made him a natural fit for the job.

"My passion in life was always animation," he says. "I was basically someone out there in the wilderness saying animation was going to come back big, we'd better all be on board."

The first significant property Walker tried to bring to the small screen was Louis Sachar's book *The Sideways Stories from Wayside School*. The idea was to have a dynamic mixed-media show with live-action elements interspersed with stop-motion. The blackboard would come alive and the pencils would speak, ideas Walker thought might make the project a successful Saturday morning series.

However, the higher-ups at CBS were disinterested, though they felt the project might be more attractive if a star were attached. CBS was still licking its wounds from *Pryor's Place*, Richard Pryor's failed children's television show produced by Sid and Marty Krofft. The show was expensive to produce and its poor ratings caused a huge financial loss to CBS. The network was reluctant to take a chance on any future properties, but executives might be willing to listen if a big enough star were attached to the project and if the show had an animated format.

As Walker was trying to brainstorm who might be a good celebrity to approach with his Wayside idea, he was invited to an advance screening of *Big Adventure* in July, a month ahead of its theatrical release. Although he was hardly a fan of the character, Walker was marginally familiar with Pee-wee Herman from his appearances on *David Letterman*. When Reubens had still been an underground star, Walker had noticed the actor's profile rising throughout the early 1980s, although he hadn't really given the character much thought. However, that changed once the film started rolling on the big screen.

© The Groundlings

"I sat through it and just thought this is the guy," Walker remembers. "I think I was more attracted to Tim Burton's view of everything than Pee-wee himself. The whole opening segment of Pee-wee getting breakfast with the contraption was just absolutely spot-on and I knew it would make for great children's programming."

Walker was also amazed by the unique stop-motion animated sequences sprinkled into the film's narrative. There was a dinosaur gnawing on a bicycle, eyeballs that shone in the night sky, and a phantom trucker named Large Marge whose face morphed from human to monster on the screen.

"It was exactly where I thought motion pictures should go and I wanted to be the first to bring that experience to television," he says.

Walker called Bill McEuen to discuss the possibility of a Pee-wee television show, but he was told by McEuen that Reubens had his sights set on being a movie star and television would be a step backwards.

"There was great reluctance at the time because when you've done a movie, doing a Saturday morning children's show isn't the next thing on your agenda," says Judy Price, then vice president of children's television at CBS.

As Reubens and his team were preparing for *Big Adventure*'s nationwide release, a team from Broadcast Arts, a New York–based animation production company run by Steve Oakes and Peter Rosenthal, flew out to Los Angeles to pitch ideas for a children's television show to the major networks. The upstart company had gained notoriety for its series of 10-second MTV station identifications while the network was in its infancy. This led to a Clio Award for excellence and creativity in advertising and design, and a new office in Manhattan with access to a large network of independent artists. Broadcast Arts landed a meeting with Walker days after he had approached Reubens.

The executive liked what he saw on their demo reel, but he became ecstatic when he recognized a Crest toothpaste ad that had attracted his attention months earlier. The ad featured a small boy walking in the darkness toward the dentist, past ominous looking trees with human-like faces, straight out of *The Wizard of Oz*. The boy walks into an old Victorian house for his dental appointment and is given a clean bill of health. The entire town erupts into happiness. The boy is treated to a convertible ride, a ticker-tape parade, and fireworks. The spot integrated various animation styles to tell a complete story in a compact period of time.

"What I liked about it was that it wasn't polished," Walker explains. "There was a crude, rustic quality to it. It wasn't Madison Avenue. It was a quirky netherworld they created through animation and the obvious collaboration of some brilliant artists."

Walker's gears started turning. He told the Broadcast Arts reps his idea and swore them to secrecy.

"I'm trying to do this show based on the Wayside School books with Pee-wee Herman," he said. "And I'd love to do it with you."

The team was instructed to come back with some animation designs that would work well in a school setting but retain a left-of-center sensibility. Within a few weeks they returned with sketches for a number of segments including food that was alive in the cafeteria fridge and a family of dinosaurs living in the science room.

"It was exactly the presentation I needed," Walker recalls. "I just had to get past Paul's agent."

The opportunity came a few weeks later at the movie premiere for *Big Adventure*. Warner Brothers had thrown a huge carnival-themed party in promotion for the film, attended by celebrities like Eddie Murphy, David Lee Roth, and Alice Cooper. The

THE STORY OF A REBEL AND HIS BIKE.

PEE-WEE HERMAN
Pee-wee's
BIG ADVENTURE

An ASPEN FILM SOCIETY / ROBERT SHAPIRO Production
PEE-WEE HERMAN • PEE-WEE'S BIG ADVENTURE
co-starring ELIZABETH DAILY • MARK HOLTON • DIANE SALINGER • JUDD OMEN music composed by DANNY ELFMAN
executive producer WILLIAM E. McEUEN written by PHIL HARTMAN & PAUL REUBENS & MICHAEL VARHOL
produced by ROBERT SHAPIRO and RICHARD GILBERT ABRAMSON directed by TIM BURTON

Courtesy Photofest / Warner Bros. © Warner Bros.

event was televised on MTV, an up-and-coming cable network that had invited Pee-wee on air several times in the preceding years.

"One of the most important aspects of Paul's success was MTV," Richard Abramson says. "In the early days of MTV, you could get anything on. It was one channel and they weren't a big corporate entity with a huge presence around the world like they are today. They were just about fun, and I worked to make Pee-wee the mascot of MTV. He would do the New Year's Eve show and other things for them and the idea was to build up enough credits with the network so that when it was time to publicize the movie, MTV would owe us. It was important to make Pee-wee hip and there was nothing more hip in the '80s than MTV. [The network was] very important in telling people it's okay to like Pee-wee."

Walker was able to get in to the premiere, but when he saw the spectacle, he knew his chances of getting Reubens involved in the TV project were slim.

"I was thinking, 'Shit, there's no way they're going to do a Saturday morning show,'" he says. "I was so frustrated because I knew I had a hit on my hands."

Despite his pessimism, Walker was able to sidestep McEuen and directly approach Abramson to speak to him about bringing Pee-wee to Saturday morning TV. He was met with another cold shoulder.

For the next several weeks, Walker continued to make regular phone calls to Abramson — none were returned. After months of unwanted solicitation, Abramson finally called Walker back to tell him that Reubens was still not interested.

"I said, 'Just let me have five minutes,'" Walker recalls. "'If I don't convince you that this is the exact right career move for you, I'll walk away from your doorstep and never darken it again.'"

Abramson agreed, and on the night before Christmas Eve, Walker met with Abramson and Reubens, armed with Broadcast Arts' designs and demo reel to make the pitch for Pee-wee Herman to join CBS. Although the response in the meeting was tepid, there was one glimmer of hope that a deal might be possible. As Walker says, "Paul looked at me and said, 'I've always wanted to do a children's show.'"

With the Christmas holidays, Hollywood went dark, and Walker sat in limbo for over a week, waiting to hear back from Reubens' team. The days felt like millennia, but when the calendar page turned to January, there was good news — Reubens was interested in working out a deal.

A meeting was set up between Reubens, Abramson, Walker, and several representatives from Broadcast Arts. While the Wayside School idea was in the forefront of Walker's mind, Reubens had other plans.

"The initial concept was for the show to be much more animation heavy and not rely on his presence, to save him from having to be on set for weeks on end," says Steve Oakes, co-founder of Broadcast Arts. "But he got into it and immersed himself in the project. He really became the centerpiece and more than just a host."

It was in this meeting that *Pee-wee's Playhouse* was born. Reubens proposed taking elements from his HBO show and modifying them for an audience of children. Where on stage the playhouse appeared small and compact, on television it would look like an expansive clubhouse. There would be plenty of opportunity for new animation produced by Broadcast Arts, but also vintage cartoons from the golden age of animation.

"The initial meetings were really quite wonderful," Oakes recalls. "We were thinking about kids' shows and we were getting nostalgic, while still being conscious of catering to the emerging style of MTV and a visually literate generation."

Although five years had passed since *The Pee-wee Herman Show*, Reubens had never totally abandoned the playhouse concept. On *Letterman* appearances he was frequently referred as a "children's show host." Pee-wee also recorded a song called "I Know You Are, But What Am I," written by stage show composer Jay Cotton, and the song reinforced the image of Pee-wee in a playhouse where no girls were allowed. Many cast members of the original stage show revisited the playhouse set in a segment of the 1982 short-lived television show *Twilight Theatre*.

"They wound up cutting everything out except what Paul did with Steve Martin," says Brian Seff, who played Mr. Jelly Donut in the original stage production. "But that wasn't Paul's fault. It was the producers'."

Walker told Judy Price about his idea and she agreed that the network should try to work out a deal with Reubens. While the star and his management were receptive to the idea, they were not totally convinced that a Saturday morning children's television show was the next logical career move. *Big Adventure* had nearly recouped its entire budget on its opening weekend and now Warner Brothers wanted a sequel. Pee-wee Herman appeared to be on a trajectory to be the country's newest, if not most unconventional, cinematic leading man. However, Walker had successfully sold Price on Reubens and the two continued the task of convincing the actor and his management to swim in the less-glamorous waters of children's television.

"I thought Paul was so creative and imaginative that I could pretty much trust him to do something totally unique and similar to his HBO show," Price explains. "I basically promised him a lot of autonomy. I wasn't going to try and take his vision and take a square peg and put it in a round hole. My argument to him was also that if he didn't do the show because he didn't like the current programming on Saturday morning, then how would it ever get better unless creative and talented people create shows for it?"

In order to seal the deal, Walker agreed to give Reubens an on-air commitment, ensuring that the show would be included in the network's fall lineup that September. The move was a bit brazen and it caused Walker some heat with his bosses.

"Those things were just not done," Walker says. "Nobody ever got that kind of commitment. It meant the show was going on television come hell or high water."

The largest remaining hurdle was financial. "We knew we were looking at a very expensive show from the beginning," Walker recalls. In order for Walker and Price to produce a mixed-media show, incorporating traditional two-dimensional animation, stop-motion animation, puppetry, and live action, they would need a sizeable budget. At the time, Saturday morning cartoon budgets were averaging $250,000 an episode. *Pee-wee's Playhouse* would require a lot more.

Ultimately, Price was able to secure a budget of a reported $325,000 an episode, although Reubens remembers the number being closer to $525,000.

"That was something I had to push through my own management," Price recalls. "That was the price tag attached to the show. Paul had some very good negotiators, but the show did have a lot of elements. It's what I had to do to let Paul see his vision through."

To provide Reubens with the money needed for the show's production, Price had to curtail the funds going to several other programs on CBS's Saturday morning lineup. The idea was that Pee-wee Herman would attract new viewers to the network and the rest of the shows would benefit in ratings, even if their budgets were constrained in the process.

With a deal firmly in place, *Pee-wee's Playhouse* was green-lit for production in February of 1986. Oakes and Rosenthal, cofounders of Broadcast Arts, quickly flew back to New York to begin assembling a crew, while Reubens gathered a team of writers and actors in Los Angeles.

PRODUCTION

The Pee-wee Herman Show and Reubens' tenure at the Groundlings had given him a head start when it came to hiring writers. He immediately enlisted the help of Michael Varhol, one of *Big Adventure*'s cowriters. John Paragon, who had been instrumental in the writing of the original live show, was also invited to join the writing team. Max Robert, a friend of Reubens, was brought on board, despite having no previous writing credits to his name. George McGrath, a struggling comedian, was pegged to be the fifth collaborator on the show's first season.

"Paul literally plucked me from the chorus to write his show," McGrath recalls. "He came to see a performance at the Groundlings and came backstage afterwards to ask who had written the scenes he liked. I guess I had written them all. A few days later he called me at home and asked me if I wanted to write a kids' show he was going to do. I had never even met him before that night at the theater. Of course, that phone call completely changed my life."

The group set up shop in a spacious high-rise office building at the corner of Sunset Boulevard and Cahuenga in Hollywood and they worked from 10 a.m. to 4 p.m. every weekday. Initially, the task was to come up with characters, running gags, and catch-phrases that would be integrated into the scripts.

George McGrath

"We came up with ideas for most of the shows and developed a basic template for the episodes," Varhol explains. "There'd be an intro, secret word, situation, cartoon, dinosaur family, et cetera."

Reubens' mornings were often consumed by conference calls with his management, CBS, and Broadcast Arts, and so the remaining four writers would work on bits individually and then regroup in the afternoon to collaborate. Eventually the operation moved to Reubens' house, an environment thought to be more conducive to creativity. The new location, however, caused a constant challenge for the writers to balance business and pleasure.

"Paul was easily distracted and enjoyed having everyone distracted when he was," McGrath recalls. "The great thing about Paul is that every word or idea didn't have to come from him. He was always happy to find that we were eight pages closer to finishing a script when he was done playing."

Despite distractions, the writers completed 13 episodes for the show's first season. Each episode was begun on a Monday, completed by that Friday, and faxed over to Broadcast Arts in New York, who would begin building the props necessary for the shoot.

Although CBS gave Reubens carte blanche when it came to his artistic vision, the creative team had a few developmental snags with the network's standards and practices department.

The connect-the-dots sequences in the Magic Screen were initially conceived to be similar in style to the children's program *Winky Dink and You*, which aired on CBS from 1953 until 1957. The show's main premise was that children at home could interact with the actors by drawing on their television screens using a transparent magic film and crayons. The vinyl plastic film,

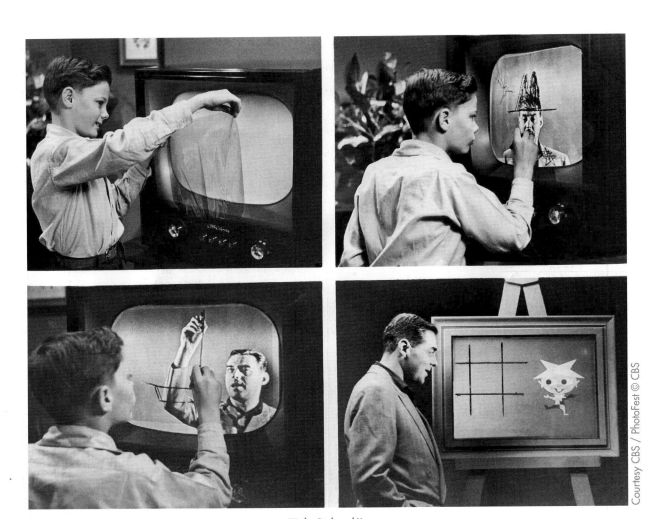

Winky Dink and You

which was called a "magic drawing screen," was available at stores for 50 cents and could be reused from week to week.

Despite Reubens' enthusiasm for inviting the viewing audience to interact with Pee-wee by connecting the dots on their television sets, the network opposed the idea.

"The broadcast standards department at CBS wouldn't allow there to be an element of the show where kids had to buy something to participate," Price remembers. "Paul managed to get some advertiser to agree to give out the magic screens for free, but our standards and practices department still wouldn't allow it. That's how it ended up being the connect-the-dots sequences done with animation."

It was decided, instead, to have a talking magic screen puppet that would simulate the *Winky Dink* experience for viewers. Alison Mork was chiefly responsible for giving the wooden

Magic Screen puppet mobility and voice. Her mouth moved by remote control, and she glided across the playhouse floor thanks to a thin wire attached to the base of her legs that was simply pulled back and forth. The multicolored "magic" that appeared in her screen was put in during post-production and so it was invisible to the cast and crew during shooting. On set, Magic Screen was filled with a large green rectangle.

The videos that were projected on the Screen were voiced by George McGrath. Although the segments appeared to be public domain videos, many were shot specifically for *Playhouse* and edited to look like 1950s educational videos.

"I would get the footage and would improvise the voiceover," McGrath remembers. "That was a lot of fun. I love those little films."

Magic Screen is most remembered because Pee-wee played connect-the-dots against her cartoon backdrops. In almost every episode, Pee-wee would jump inside, release a handful of dots from his pocket, connect them with magical lines that would transform into an animated object, and then Pee-wee would interact with the animation. Editor Glenn Lazzaro worked on compositing the first season's connect-the-dots animations.

© John Duke Kisch / CBS

"It's every kid's dream to jump into an Etch A Sketch or TV set," Lazzaro says.

Although the connect-the-dots segments were brief on television, several days of pains-taking work went into creating each one for the viewing audience. First, Reubens would be shot in costume against a green screen. The editors and animators would use a digital recorder to construct the animated landscape around the actor. Constructing just one 45-second seg-ment would take several days.

"I think it was a whole weekend," Lazzaro remembers. "I think we would come in on Saturday morning at nine and finish sometime around eleven on Sunday. Sometimes we would stay overnight and sleep in the editing room."

The time spent on the sequences paid off, as the connect-the-dots sequence, along with Pee-wee's accompanying song, is one of the most memorable aspects of the show's run.

The only other significant run-in Reubens had with the network censors came during production on the first episode. The script called for Pee-wee to make an animal out of a potato by sticking pencils in it, but the network feared it was insensitive to waste food.

"As associate producer on the first season, I was sort of the liaison between Paul and the network," says Scott Chester, who was Richard Abramson's assistant. "I'd come to him with these notes like, 'The network doesn't want you to put pencils in potatoes because they don't want kids to become upset if they don't have access to them.' Paul just looked at me and went, 'Wait, so they can afford televisions, but not potatoes?'"

Judy Price, VP of children's programming at the time, thought the network's reaction was a bit overblown, but she understood the reasoning. "They were thinking of the starving children. Ultimately, Paul won that battle."

Strangely, the one battle that Reubens and the writers didn't have to wage against standards and practices was over the show's occasionally adult humor. The character of Miss Yvonne, for example, with her propensity for hitting on nearly every male in Puppetland, was immune from any criticism from the network. Despite her perceived pursuit of sex, Lynne Stewart maintains that her character's intentions were often more innocent than they appeared.

"I think Miss Yvonne's goal was to kiss," Stewart explains. "It was very important to her to kiss as many men as possible, but I truly feel she was a virgin."

© John Duke Kisch / CBS

ASSEMBLING THE ARTISTS

On the other coast, Broadcast Arts was building their own team to spearhead the animation and production aspects of the upcoming shoot. Prudence Fenton, who had been instrumental in the company's production of many MTV network IDs, was hired as producer of animation and effects. Throughout the spring, she began looking for talent at the company and in the New York freelance artist community to bring *Pee-wee's Playhouse* to life.

She collected hundreds of sketches and shipped them to Los Angeles for Reubens' feedback, but very little was approved.

"Paul kept saying, 'I like it, but it's not what I'm looking for,'" says Phil Trumbo, an animation director for the first season. "I knew that Gary Panter designed the HBO special, and that sensibility was really what Paul was looking for. There was a certain sense at Broadcast Arts that we were creative and should be able to do it, but at a certain point, if you're looking for a van Gogh, you'd better get van Gogh."

Broadcast Arts put in a call to Panter, who agreed to join the production. He was not only instrumental in sparking new creativity, but he also brought Wayne White and Ric Heitzman on as art directors. The three became their own unit, working out of the Broadcast Arts headquarters, but marching to the beat of their own drummer.

Within weeks, Panter expanded upon his live-show set design and created a visually appealing clubhouse for Pee-wee and his pals to play in. The cubist, seafoam green door was replaced with a red door that looked both sharp and comfortable to the touch. Jambi's gray box was bejeweled and painted a glittery shade of violet. The walls were all given a complete renovation, with funky patterns and vibrant colors as far as the eye could see.

Although Panter had created the look of the puppets for the original stage production, White and Heitzman were chiefly responsible for designing the puppets for television. The duo's unique sensibility and approach paid dividends when it came to creating an original look for children's television.

"We'd been doing these weirdo puppet shows for years in art school," White recalls. "Oddly enough, this Pee-wee Herman concept came along and fit us perfectly. We were thinking psychedelic. We weren't thinking 'kid show.' We were thinking of blowing people's minds."

Pterry-Dactyl, whose name was shortened to Pterri, was one of two puppets from *The Pee-wee Herman Show* to make it to the *Playhouse*. In addition to the abbreviated forename, his character was changed from Kap'n Karl's rough-and-tumble dinosaur companion to Pee-wee's loveably insecure pet, and it was once again voiced by John Paragon. Three different Pterri puppets were used during the show's run. The first was a marionette puppet on two strings that would be operated high above the playhouse set. The second was a rod puppet, similar to the kind used in the 1981 stage show, and the last was a hand puppet. All three versions of Pterri were between 16 and 18 inches tall.

Greg Harrison lent a hand to operate Mr. Knucklehead, the other character from the live show to make it to Saturday morning. Although he had been a crude sock puppet in 1981, the character was reconceived as a giant fist with googly eyes and a mouth drawn on in lipstick that told bad knock-knock jokes.

One of the new puppets designed specifically for the TV show was Conky 2000. With his junkyard-salvage body (consisting of a typewriter, turntable, and an old boom box), the character was designed to be a contemporary homage to classic science fiction shows like *The Twilight Zone* and *Lost in Space*. His primary function was to give Pee-wee the secret word at the beginning of each episode.

Conky's look was designed by puppeteer Greg Harrison, who also portrayed the character during the show's first season. According to George McGrath, Harrison was a natural first-choice for being inside the Conky suit.

"Greg was set from the beginning because he built the puppet and knew his ins and outs," McGrath recalls. "He was also willing to get into that very uncomfortable contraption and stay inside for hours on end in the incredible heat."

Animation director Dave Powers, who created the sound effects for the show's animated sequences, remembers the unusual way in which Conky found his voice.

"They had brought in Mark Mothersbaugh from Devo to do the voice live with a lot of sound equipment," he recalls. "But somehow this didn't work. I took the opportunity to make a tape of robot voices for Paul. I was scared to death. This was the first time I visited the set, Paul was getting his makeup done, and everyone was watching me walk in with my boom box and play this tape of robot voices."

Reubens didn't approve any of the voices. Undeterred, Powers asked for a second chance. After filming wrapped that day, the two joined Greg Harrison, went to Reubens' rented Manhattan apartment, and listened to a recording of a Stevie Wonder song that incorporated electronic voices. Powers returned to his SoHo apartment, where he had sound equipment, and worked on a new demo tape, which was approved in the morning and became the template for Conky's voice.

With their quick wit and occasionally dour attitude, Pee-wee's talking fish, which were operated using two big metal handles that protruded from the back of the tank, were the playhouse equivalent of the Muppets' Statler and Waldorf. Their primary function in the show remained consistent throughout the run of the series: the purple fish, voiced by Ric Heitzman, would make an observation about something going on in the playhouse, and the yellow fish, voiced by George McGrath, would follow up with a sardonic punch line.

Another new character was Mr. Kite, the playhouse weatherman. Lying on the floor in front of a blue screen, and with a camera positioned several feet above the ground so that his body was concealed, Wayne White provided the voice and movement for the character's scenes. The Puppetland backdrops were added in postproduction to make it appear as if the character was soaring high above the playhouse.

Ric Heitzman provided the voice and movement for Mr. Window, Pee-wee's canary colored friend who served as the playhouse doorman. To make this puppet move, Heitzman would lie on his back outside the playhouse set, using one arm to control a large lever that gave the mouth movement. His other arm would be on a giant dowel that would allow him to control the eye movement.

Of all of the new puppets, none were cooler than the beatnik Puppetland Band made up of Dirty Dog, Cool Cat, and Chicky Baby. Set against a backdrop of an alleyway, the trio performed jazz music, made abstract art, and spoke in rhymes that would make Gwendolyn Brooks and Jack Kerouac proud.

Wayne White controls Mr. Kite;
(below) Ric Heitzman operates Mr. Window

Wayne White and Alison Mork

© John Duke Kisch / CBS

© George McGrath

Allison Mork and Chairry

Dirty Dog, the bowler hat–wearing blue hound voiced by Wayne White, provided the bass, while Cool Cat, a feline in oversized sunglasses voiced by Ric Heitzman, tapped out steady beats on the bongos. Chicky Baby, with stringy blond hair covering one of her permanently closed eyes, was on vocals, which were provided by Alison Mork.

Randy, the mischievous marionette, was conceived as a subversive contemporary response to Howdy Doody, according to puppeteer Wayne White, who also provided the character's voice. By comparing Randy and Howdy side-by-side, one can see how White was inspired by the classic character and in which ways he updated him for a new generation. Randy had maintained Howdy's freckles and red hair, but Howdy's slick hair style was traded in for a high-top buzz cut. Gone was Howdy's cowboy clothing, replaced by a white t-shirt and jeans, reminiscent of 1950s greasers like James Dean in *Rebel Without a Cause* and John Travolta in *Grease*.

With the arguable exception of Randy, the door-to-door salesman was the undeniable antagonist of the show's first season. With his too-large head resting atop his too-small body, his physical presence alone was enough for Pee-wee to slam his vinyl red door and scream really loud with horror. Ric Heitzman was the man inside the salesman's oversized, mascot-inspired costume, and he played the role with the rigidity of your typical unsuccessful traveling salesman.

There is no playhouse puppet more beloved and remembered than Chairry, Pee-wee's overstuffed seafoam blue armchair voiced and operated by Alison Mork. The puppet was backless, which allowed Mork room to sit atop a sand bag. She would inch her way into the puppet and, once inside, her arms slid into the puppet's. There was a foot pedal used to operate Chairry's mouth and wooden dowels to control her eye movements.

When creating the look of the puppets, the creative team sought to stake their claim with other popular children's entertainment of the day. "I brought a very anti-Muppet stance to the whole project," White says.

"We were also cartoonists and that cartoon-vibe runs through the show," Heitzman explains.

Steve Oakes at Broadcast Arts had called on reinforcements from Aardman Studios in England to animate the Penny cartoons. "We didn't know much about the project," Nick Park recalls. "We were told what the assignment was and got to it."

Kent Burton animates the Dinosaur Family

According to Richard Goleszowski, an animator from the show's first season known to most as Golly, the creation of Penny was an international collaborative process.

"Penny was Paul's idea," he recalls. "His initial idea was to do a classical cartoon that looked like it was made in the 1930s. He had this idea for a character with pennies for eyes."

Despite the initial idea, Reubens and the production team at Broadcast Arts were undecided on how she should look.

"They sent over some of Gary Panter's designs to England for us to get inspired and it was quite a shock," Golly remembers. "We weren't used to that style of American underground comic art. Instead, Nick Park decided to send over some sketches of Penny in a Wallace and Gromit style. Paul was happy, and we flew out to America to get started."

In order to achieve the stream-of-consciousness narration for the cartoons, dozens of preteen girls were given large glasses of Coca-Cola and were asked to talk freely about whatever interested them. The process gave the animators the freedom to create a script and animate on the fly.

"It's a very creative thing to do, to animate like that, because you have to find a story through all of the narration," Golly says. "It makes the process more creative because you have to find a way to make it work."

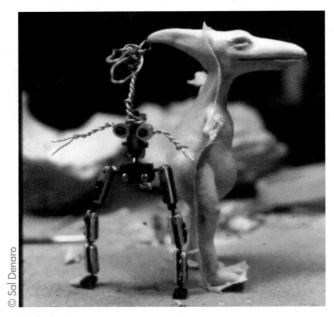

The dinosaurs being constructed

However, the young girls' chatter covered some ground the animators simply couldn't use, which created a surprising problem. "Whitney Houston was a massive star in the summer of 1986 and it seemed she was every little girl's hero," Golly remembers. "We had hours of tape of kids going on about how much they loved her."

After animating 10 Penny cartoons, the "Aardmans" were called back to England. Broadcast Arts animator Dave Daniels took up the responsibility of finishing the remaining three cartoons.

"The thing I tried to do was emulate their style as much as possible," he says. "I spent several days studying what they had already done with Penny. I was trying to throw away my individual look. I just thought about it as an actor would. When you go on stage, you're trying to throw yourself completely into a part. That's what I was trying to do with Penny."

Despite his best efforts, Daniels' style came through on the segments he animated. Careful observers may notice variation in the look and style of the Penny cartoons during the first season.

"I tended to have a little more of a speedy, Warner Brothers animation style to it, which isn't necessarily good because there's an understated subtlety to the Aardman stuff," Daniels says. "They brought a lot of really small, nice touches to it. My style was more active and more American, but theirs were filled with more dry wit and restraint. I think theirs are better, to be frank, but I tried really hard to follow their rules and not do my own thing."

The dinosaur family sequences in the first season were animated by Kent Burton, and it was Burton who had come up with the initial concept during a brainstorming session with the production team.

"I thought that maybe Pee-wee could have a time machine and would go back to the days of the dinosaurs," he says. "I wanted them to be realistic and do dinosaur sorts of things. I thought it would be a good education for the kids to learn about prehistoric times. The producers liked the idea of dinosaurs but they wanted it to be playful, so they came up with a whole mouse-hole concept, with dinosaurs that looked like toys. That was fine with me. What meant a lot was that I asked for dinosaurs and they gave them to me — which was great after suffering through so many boring commercials I was used to animating."

Burton also helped design and physically sculpt the latex figurines that he used to animate the sequences.

"I had the idea of putting pterodactyl heads on them," he says. "And although I didn't design the mother and father, I sculpted them. We knew that we wanted the dinosaurs to be upright and have tails, so the designs kind of came together naturally."

The dinosaurs, like the food items in the refrigerator, were constructed using metal armatures on which dino skins were stretched, similar to the way the gorilla was constructed for the original *King Kong* film. The metal skeletons for the dinosaur family were constructed by Sal Denaro, who was left uncredited for his work.

Stephen R. Johnson, director of Peter Gabriel's "Sledgehammer" video, was brought on board to direct the series. His MTV directing style greatly enhanced the look of the show, although his lack of planning before shoots frequently caused delays.

"He was very much in charge," Golly recalls. "He'd be very dramatic and loud. He'd change things at the drop of a hat. It was very exciting working with him, but he'd always be getting in arguments with the producers."

Art director Sid Bartholomew and *Playhouse* guest star Calvert DeForest

© John Duke Kisch / CBS

CREATING THE CAST

The job of casting *Pee-wee's Playhouse* posed some early problems. While an ensemble of actors was already in place from *The Pee-wee Herman Show*, not all were invited to join Reubens on his Saturday morning TV show. Lynne Stewart, Phil Hartman, and John Paragon were asked to reprise their roles, but the remaining members were not asked to come over and play. Although the personalities of his character remained unchanged, the spelling of Kap'n Karl's name was changed to the more traditional "Captain Carl." Stewart and Paragon signed on right away, but Hartman took more convincing.

"There was a lot of jealousy between Paul and Phil," Richard Abramson explains. "They were close friends, but Paul never really went out of his way to help Phil in his career, and Phil felt like he was always in Paul's shadow. In a way, he was."

After the release of *Pee-wee's Big Adventure* and before filming had begun on *Playhouse*, Reubens was invited to host *Saturday Night Live* as Pee-wee. To make certain the character was written into sketches that would work for his unique sense of humor, Abramson convinced Lorne Michaels to allow Hartman and John Paragon to join the show's writers for the episode Pee-wee hosted. Michaels agreed.

"I don't know if that's ever happened before or since," Abramson says.

When *Saturday Night Live* was casting for its following season, Hartman decided to audition. At the time he was a regular on *Pee-wee's Playhouse*. He asked Abramson to put in a telephone call to Michaels in advance of his audition to help his chances of getting on the show. Abramson did, and within weeks, Hartman was hired. But the SNL schedule limited his accessibility to Reubens and ensured he would only be able to

© John Duke Kisch / CBS

play Captain Carl for one season. According to McGrath, Reubens felt Hartman's departure from *Playhouse* showed disloyalty. News that Hartman's focus had shifted to another project put a permanent damper on his relationship with Reubens.

"Paul actually was angry about this, rather than happy for Phil's success," he says. "He was really nasty to Phil and felt the reason he got the job was because Paul [had originally] brought him there as a writer. They didn't speak for years."

Although several Groundlings joined Pee-wee on Saturday morning, there are several factors that led to others not being invited to move to New York, among them that the original cast of the stage show had almost no ethnic diversity. Reubens wanted the program to more closely reflect the viewing audience, so changes were made to incorporate more people

of color into the cast. According to Richard Abramson, it was important to Reubens that the playhouse be a place where people of all backgrounds could feel at home.

"Both Paul and I grew up in a situation where we were a little bit of outcasts growing up, especially in grade school where I was the only Jewish kid," he explains. "That's why the main idea behind *Pee-wee's Playhouse* was that you don't have to be the coolest and best-looking kid on the playground to still have friends. You can be different and still be successful. That's the way the show was designed."

To increase the diversity of the show, John Moody's Mailman Mike was replaced by S. Epatha Merkerson as Reba the Mail Lady. Merkerson was a relatively unknown actress who had just landed a small role in Spike Lee's *She's Gotta Have It.*

Johann Carlo and Pee-wee

© John Duke Kisch / CBS

"It was one of those wild things where I went to audition and I thought I was funny and the person I auditioned for didn't," Merkerson recalls. "And so I had blown the job. And I guess weeks later they got new casting people."

Gilbert Lewis and Johann Carlo were cast in the newly created roles of the King of Cartoons and Dixie the Cab Driver, respectively.

In between filming projects, Reubens would often grow his hair out past his shoulders and sport a goatee. Although he was never photographed without his classic crew-cut while dressed as Pee-wee, many of his friends and associates were used to seeing Reubens with long locks and facial hair. "When I went in to audition, I didn't realize his name was Paul Reubens," Carlo remembers. "I asked him where Pee-wee was. I saw Paul, but with his long, stringy hair he kind of looked like a hippie. I thought he was a producer."

With the majority of the cast in place, the production hit two major casting problems. Dozens of people had auditioned for the role of Cowboy Curtis, but no one worked.

"They brought in all these models," Reubens recalls. "Guys who were great looking and weren't right."

After a day of casting, Reubens remembered that Larry Fishburne, who was a friend of the spotlight operator for *The Pee-wee Herman Show* at the Groundlings, was in New York.

"I called him up and said, 'Will you come down and read this?' and we cast him like thirty seconds later," Reubens recalls.

"I was there when he interviewed," says Kevin Ladson, a production assistant on the show's first season. "I said, 'You're Larry Fishburne from *Apocalypse Now* and *The Cotton Club*!' and he said, 'Yes sirree!' He had the accent and he came full-on in character."

For the role of Mrs. Steve, the snooping next-door neighbor, Reubens wanted Suzanne Kent, a Groundling alumna.

© John Duke Kisch / CBS

Larry Fishburne

Despite her interest, she was unable to join the *Playhouse* cast.

"I wanted to do *Pee-wee*, but it was a timing issue with *It's Garry Shandling's Show*," Kent recalls. "I couldn't do both, and I guess my agent had committed to Garry Shandling first."

The role ultimately went to Shirley Stoler, a character actress best known for her starring role in *The Honeymoon Killers*. It was a concession that Reubens was forced to make and one that he remained unhappy with for the duration of the shoot because Stoler was a deeply polarizing presence on the set.

"Shirley was probably the laziest actress I've ever worked with," McGrath says. "When she was supposed to play ring-around-the-rosey with the kids, she stood in one spot and flapped her arms. If she was ever placed near furniture or a window ledge, she would try to sit down. She was always whining and had a really low, negative energy. She kept complaining that she was 'drowning in her own moisture,' which only made everyone near her more aware of the heat."

Despite McGrath's assessment, Stoler's on-set attitude was a source of amusement to many others. Kevin Ladson was in charge of making the coffee, in addition to his other responsibilities. One day his busy schedule led to a memorable interaction with Stoler.

"I didn't change the coffee pot for at least nine hours," he recalls. "As I was going to change the coffee, Shirley insisted that I get her a cup. I looked at it and it was beyond mud. I told her it was totally undrinkable and she said, 'Just give me what's there.' I went back and forth with her a few times, but she insisted on getting a cup right then and there. I poured her a cup and she wanted it black, with just a little Sweet 'N Low. She drank the muddy coffee and said, 'Mmmm! This is the best coffee I've ever had!'"

Shirley Stoler flips the bird on the *Playhouse* set

© John Duke Kisch / CBS

DESIGNING THE OPENING

To film the episodes, Broadcast Arts rented a SoHo loft that had been used previously as a sweatshop. Before construction could begin on the set, the entire space had to be gutted and cleared of sewing machine tables and spinning wheels.

"It was quite funky, but suited our needs," Steve Oakes explains. "It was a wonderful hole in the wall. We converted it into a stage, but it was sort of a flophouse. Pee-wee's flophouse."

Although the space was large enough to film in, the conditions were less than desirable.

"This little production company was not fit to produce a mixed-media live-action show," Prudence Fenton recalls. "They wouldn't even rent a real stage. The space didn't even have enough electricity to supply all the lights. Every fifteen feet there'd be a pole to hold up the loft ceiling, so the set had to be designed around them. The stage was on the fifth floor and we had this huge air conditioning truck we called 'Airy' feeding cold air in from downstairs because Paul liked it cold. He'd be in the suit and everyone else would literally be in down jackets."

As shooting began on the live-action set, producer Fenton and animator Phil Trumbo began working on the show's opening title sequence, an amalgamation of animation, live-action, and special effects, designed to establish the colorfully unpredictable world that the viewing audience was soon to encounter.

Work on the opening began in early July. According to Trumbo, who directed the animation portion, Reubens had a very specific concept in mind. "He wanted it to feel sort of like you're coming out of a national park," Trumbo says. "He wanted the funky sign, and the camera to come across this place that looks like outsider art or some weird roadside attraction filled with all these wacky characters. Then the camera would go into that place."

After meeting with Reubens to discuss his vision, Trumbo storyboarded the sequence. He and Fenton split the animators

© Richard Kent Burton

The camera set-up for shooting the beginning shot of the opening credits

into two groups, with half working on the exterior model for the playhouse and the rest working to create the fantasy forest landscape through which the camera navigates before arriving at the playhouse door.

When storyboarding was completed and the set designed, Trumbo and Fenton began preliminary test shots on the animated sequence. Initially, their tests failed to match up with Reubens' concept.

"I would work out the moves and show it to Paul in a rough state before we did all of the animation," Trumbo says. "I want to say we did about twenty versions of it before we had a basic move that he liked. At one point, when we both were getting frustrated, I got a camcorder and said, 'Geez, will you just take this around the set and give me an idea what you're looking for? I feel like we're trying to give you something and we're not accomplishing what your vision is.' He literally took this big camcorder and wandered around the set with it. He didn't produce anything that helpful, but it was important to say, 'We want to do your vision but we're not quite sure how to accomplish it. How do we do that?'"

Despite the tedious approval process caused by Reubens' perfectionism, Fenton feels his feedback significantly enhanced the final product. "We showed him that move every day for seven weeks, twice a day, and every time he made a suggestion it always made it better," Fenton says. "But it was a lengthy process."

The seven-week routine finally came to an end when Trumbo joined forces with Devo lead singer Mark Mothersbaugh, who was going through a similar process with Reubens composing the theme music. They ran into one another on the *Playhouse* set.

"Mark and I were waiting to see Paul at the same time," Trumbo says. "As we were waiting, we talked about what we were doing, and Mark was going through the same revision process with the music. Paul just wasn't hearing what he wanted. When we got into Paul's dressing room, I put in my black-and-white animatic of [our] latest opening sequence motion test. Paul had a boombox and a VHS player. I told Mark to cue up his audio and, when I signaled, we'd both push play. I said 'go' and pushed play on the visuals. Mark pushed play on the audio and we played the music and the visuals together. It looked really cool and Paul said, 'Yeah, these both look cool. Go ahead.' It was kind of like, hearing the music and seeing the picture together, it made sense to him."

After gaining approval for music (which incorporates the theme and animal sounds from Martin Denny's cover of Les Baxter's "Quiet Village"), Mothersbaugh went to work on the final version. Trumbo and Fenton worked with the animators from Broadcast Arts to complete their portion of the opening titles.

Kent Burton animates Pee-wee entering his playhouse

The long test approval process gave way to an easy shoot for the final sequence. "When we went to shoot it, I don't think we really had to do any re-shoots," Fenton says. "We had the camera move right and knew exactly what was going on. The only hard thing was that the animators stayed up for twenty hours to finish it."

Kent Burton was the lead animator on the first portion of the animated sequence. The first image the viewer sees, the sign for the playhouse, was designed by John DeFazio, while Barbara Gallucci, formerly of Industrial Light and Magic, constructed most of the clay forest. To make the trees drop during the first portion, Burton rigged the trees to wires. This enabled him to suspend the trees in the air while he moved them gradually frame-by-frame to create the illusion of falling.

The second portion of the opening sequence was animated by Dave Daniels, and this one posed more technical challenges. Not only were there more animals, with white rabbits and squirrels moving through the landscape, but also, as the playhouse came into frame, more animation was required to establish it as a place where — as the lyrics to the theme song state — anything could happen. Out-side the playhouse, deer swayed to music, a penguin revolved on the roof, and an inflatable toy created ripples in Pee-wee's above-ground pool. To animate these additional elements in a timely manner, more members of the animation team were brought in to assist Daniels. Kent Burton contributed the blue-screen birds, and Trumbo

added the digital composite shot of the live-action Pee-wee giggling before the transition into the third segment.

In the final segment, animated by both Burton and Daniels, the camera pans around the playhouse, emphasizing the animated windmill, the snowman, the bucking bronco, and the Sphinx head on the house's exterior. According to Trumbo, the model for the playhouse was between 20 and 30 feet in diameter and took up the majority of the studio where the sequence was animated. Sharp observers will notice a few differences between the model and the actual live-action set, like the absence of greenery around the flowers.

The multitude of moving objects posed some unique problems for Burton. "We never used frame grabbers [when animating] like everyone uses nowadays, where you can record every frame and flip back and forth to see what you just did," Burton recalls. "We had to remember everything." In fact, Burton's memory failed him when animating one prominent element on the playhouse model.

"If you look at the barber pole, you'll see it switches directions constantly," Burton says. "I don't mind because it was such a wacky show, but that was actually me forgetting which way I was turning it."

The animated model for Pee-wee Herman, designed by Jeff Raum, also posed an animating problem. After the model walked across the playhouse deck, camera operator J. Reid Paul pushed in with his camera. Because of the limited space between the camera and the playhouse model, Burton had to animate the last few frames blindly, relying on faith that the finished product would be acceptable. Luckily, it was.

After animation was completed, Trumbo made his way back to Reubens' dressing room for approval. "By the time we animated the sequence, it was August," Trumbo says. "The show was supposed to air in September. We were really down to the wire on this thing. I brought the completed sequence down to the set. [Paul] had an old-fashioned Moviola projector set up on his desk so he could look at dailies from each day's shoot. We ran the sequence on that. He gave his final approval and said, 'I bet you thought I'd never approve that,' referring to the endless hell of revisions. My reaction was 'Well, the show has to go on in two weeks, you would have to approve it eventually.'"

If the revision process for the animation and music was hell, the process of writing the lyrics was absolute heaven. The show's memorable theme song, sung with pitch-perfect pop perfection by Cyndi Lauper, was written from soup to nuts in less than a day.

George McGrath, who cowrote the lyrics with Reubens, remembers his first meeting to discuss the song.

"One day on the set, Paul asked me to come into his dressing room," he says. "He said he wanted the theme song to have an old-style razzmatazz feeling. He may have mentioned that he wanted the person singing to sound like Betty Boop. He went on to sing the first line in a raspy voice with jazz hands and wiggling hips. He said ideally the lyrics would mention all of the puppets."

After that day's shooting, McGrath went back to his hotel room and wrote the first draft of the lyrics on a sheet of legal paper. Barring a few minor changes that were made at a later time, the show's memorable theme song was complete.

The next day, McGrath showed Reubens the lyrics he had written. Reubens liked it and the two sang the lyrics together into a tape recorder. The tape was sent to Mothersbaugh, who composed and then submitted a sample track that closely resembled the tape he'd received. "We were both a little surprised when his track came back and it was the same tune we sang," McGrath says. "I think we thought he was going to make a new tune and just use our tune as a guide to the flavor Paul was looking for."

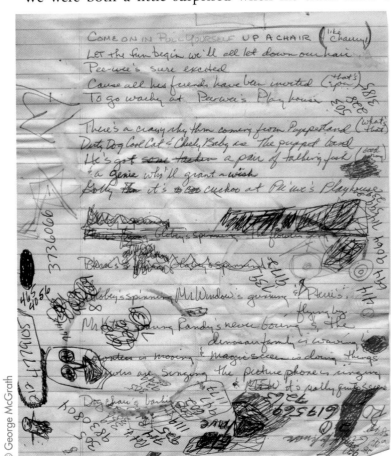
The handwritten first draft of the *Playhouse* theme song

Reubens asked Cyndi Lauper to sing the lyrics in a style that had become her signature after the success of "Girls Just Want to Have Fun." However, to Reubens' surprise and disappointment, Lauper declined the offer. Instead, she suggested Reubens use one of her backup singers, Ellen Shaw. "Cyndi wanted to be taken more seriously as a singer," McGrath says. "She was transitioning from her 'Girls Just Want to Have Fun' image to her 'True Colors' image."

The theme song was recorded at CBS on 57th Street.

Lauper came to the recording session with hopes of being able to coach Shaw into singing in Lauper's style. According to McGrath, after several attempts, it was apparent that the backup singer was having difficulty reproducing Cyndi's inimitable style. Paul convinced Lauper to record the track for him as a personal favor, and he agreed to credit Shaw as the vocalist.

The final product clocked in at two-and-a-half minutes, almost double the average run time for television theme songs. For their efforts, Trumbo and Fenton earned Daytime Emmy Awards for Outstanding Achievement and Title Design in 1987. The sequence even impressed Steve Oakes, who remains deeply proud of it to this day.

"You never get tired of looking at that opening," he says.

SHOWTIME

Pee-wee's Playhouse was scheduled to debut on CBS as part of a brand-new Saturday morning lineup at 10 a.m. on September 13, 1986. Recognizing that the program might stand out like a sore thumb in comparison to the rest of the shows broadcast on the network, Michael Chase Walker designed a schedule on the premise that *Playhouse* would be successful and that children would stick around to watch *Teen Wolf* and *Galaxy High School*, two new programs that had an edgy animation style and sensibility. It was a risky strategy, but one that CBS was willing to try.

"They were so in the ratings gutter that Judy Price basically gave me a free hand," Walker explains.

Even with a new lineup, CBS faced a serious challenge in attracting viewers to *Playhouse*, mostly because the advertising opportunities were very limited. It couldn't broadcast commercials on rival networks and CBS's own primetime lineup didn't allow for any opportunities to advertise their Saturday morning shows, as the primetime demographic didn't include young children or even their parents. Interestingly, Walker suggested advertising the children's television schedule in AMC movie theaters, a now-standard practice that was unheard of in the mid-'80s. Instead, the network decided to trust the mantra that "if you build it, they will come."

Playhouse's first airing was the ratings equivalent to a tree falling in the forest. "I had this spectacular, really creative, dynamic Saturday morning lineup, but nobody to show it to," Walker says. CBS remained in third place, trailing behind NBC's *The Smurfs* and ABC's *The Real Ghostbusters*.

Walker bore the brunt of the heat at the network, which caused minor tension between him and his bosses.

"I had gone from being this hotshot genius of Saturday morning to this pariah," he recalls. "It was clear my days were numbered. I was being called on the carpet constantly for having my lineup fail so disastrously."

Under increased stress and disappointed by the ratings, Walker resigned from the network only weeks into the new season.

However, as tensions were rising at the network, the tide was starting to turn in *Pee-wee*'s favor. An onslaught of positive press and word of mouth began to bring more adults to Saturday morning television. Although adults were not the target audience, and were considered worthless viewers as far as the advertisers were concerned, they were bringing their children, nieces, and nephews to the show. Within weeks, the show started climbing in the ratings, ultimately surpassing *The Smurfs* before the first season concluded.

Michael Chase Walker remembers *Playhouse*'s slow ascent to the top of the ratings chart as a primary reason why he left. But Judy Price has no recollection of the network being unhappy with the show in its early days.

"I don't recall, and can't really believe, that Michael was called on the carpet for any ratings deficiency," she says. "It's not uncommon for a show to start off low and build from there. We all wish for a blockbuster, but that's the exception, not the rule. Few shows ever explode out of the gate. Ratings or not, a show that creates buzz like *Pee-wee's Playhouse* did is worth its weight in gold. It was the hippest show on the air."

Within weeks of the show's debut, CBS was being heralded in the media as a frontrunner in producing innovative children's entertainment. Other television networks would have to alter their programming to compete or risk being left in CBS's dust.

"My goal was never to mount a Saturday morning revolution," Price says. "I wish I could say I was that much of a visionary. The goal was to try and find something that was new and exciting. CBS needed a show to breathe fresh air into what had become a very controlled Saturday morning environment."

The success Reubens had achieved with *Big Adventure* simply multiplied when *Playhouse* hit the air. The network requested two more seasons of the new hit show. This time, without hesitation, Reubens obliged.

While the nation was quickly catching Pee-wee fever, those involved in the original production were split in their reaction to the concept's transition from an homage to children's shows for adults to an actual program for children.

"You could put a stopwatch to episode after episode and there would be no variance," Dawna Kaufmann, executive in charge of production on *The Pee-wee Herman Show*, says. "The secret word was in the same place every time. It was all just rote and that's never what I envisioned."

"The original show was funny because it was a children's show for baby boomers who needed to talk to their inner child on a more mature level," says Guy Pohlman, a crew member on *The Pee-wee Herman Show*. "I think the children's show lost some of those elements."

However, Monica Ganas, who played Mrs. Jelly Donut in the original production, was pleased with the accomplishments of the children's show.

"It was different in substance, but not in kind," she says. "It was very artistic. I was extremely proud to have been a part of something that gave way to something *that* iconic."

The first season crew of the *Playhouse*

3 | PUPPETLAND, CALIFORNIA

DESPITE THE NATION'S enthusiasm for *Pee-wee's Playhouse*, Paul Reubens still wanted to make films. When shooting wrapped for the first season in the summer of 1986, the star approached writer George McGrath with an offer.

"Paul felt I made an important contribution creatively to the *Playhouse* and I think he found me easy to work with and fun to be around," McGrath recalls. "After the first season, he asked me to write the second season with him, and, the same day, he asked me if I wanted to cowrite a circus movie with him."

Unbeknownst to McGrath, Reubens had started fleshing out ideas a year earlier for his second feature — and he had intended to work with a different set of collaborators.

Michael Varhol had cowritten *Big Adventure* and the first season of *Playhouse*. "The Christmas after *Big Adventure*, I received a Ringling Brothers Circus postcard from Paul in Sarasota with the words 'Hint, Hint, Hint! Shhh!!!' written on the back," says Varhol. "His next film was going to be a circus story and he invited me to write it with him. I thought it was a fantastic idea and was very excited. It was a great Christmas present."

According to Varhol, the duo, along with John Paragon, began working on the still-untitled circus movie in January of the following year and continued to do so for three months. During that time, the deal on the first season of *Playhouse* was brokered, so writing on the film stopped as Reubens focused on television.

"In the twelve weeks John Paragon, Paul, and I worked on the circus project, we were trying to find the story," Varhol explains. "We screened every circus film ever made but hadn't settled on a premise. John developed the notion that Pee-wee at the circus would be too confining and claustrophobic, and that it needed to be opened up like a stage play being adapted for a film. He thought we needed to get Pee-wee away from the circus. I was strongly for

a pure circus story, with the plot involving circus characters, and that we should use the circus as a world Pee-wee enters, learns something from, and exits an unlikely hero. Paul also wanted to have an element of Americana in the story. That, and John's insistence that we needed to get away from the circus, led to Paul's resurrecting ideas from the pitch that he, Phil, and I had made for the original version of *Big Adventure*."

Before settling on the bicycle road-trip quest concept for *Pee-wee's Big Adventure*, Reubens, Phil Hartman, and Varhol had written a version of the script that was a pseudo-adaptation of Disney's *Pollyanna*. In this story, Pee-wee injects a much needed dose of sunshine into a lifeless town. Although this film never materialized, Reubens hoped to revisit many of the ideas from this draft as he developed his circus feature.

"This led to talk about Pee-wee owning a farm, inventing wild new vegetables, and a tornado blowing a circus onto his property, which is where we left off when the *Playhouse* assignment came up."

Although Warner Brothers executives were initially excited about the idea of releasing a second Pee-wee feature, they passed on the idea, thanks to Reubens' inflated salary request and their own fears that a circus movie would be a harder sell to the public than *Big Adventure* had been. Reubens made a plea to his former agent Doug Draizin for assistance in getting the film produced.

"I was working as a film executive at Lorimar Studios," Draizin recalls. "And Paul called me, told me about the situation with Warner Brothers, and asked if I was interested in doing the *Big Top*."

Draizin brought Paul in to a pitch meeting with Jerry Weintraub, who was the head of United Artists, but Weintraub was unenthusiastic about the project and declined to produce it.

Luckily for Reubens, the third time was a charm. Paramount Studios, which had passed on an early version of *Big Adventure* written by Reubens and Gary Panter, liked the concept and signed the star to a three-movie development deal.

Just as the film seemed on the right track, further derailments occurred.

"Shortly after the first season, Paul fired his managers and producers," Michael Varhol recalls. "Unfortunately, my relationship with him was part of that fallout."

Richard Abramson explains that a number of factors led to the dissolution of his business relationship with Reubens.

"I think what happened resulted out of Paul being unhappy with the conditions of the *Playhouse*," he says. "That's show business. Everyone acts in their own self interest, whether it's Paul or anyone else. As long as he had a reason to do what he did, he thought it was the right thing to do. I don't agree, but he's entitled to his opinion. There have been a couple of times in my life where everything went the way it was supposed to and I still ended up fucked."

According to George McGrath, Paragon and Reubens' relationship became rocky at around the same time, which contributed to Paragon being removed from the project.

"John and Paul have had a long history of ups and downs," McGrath explains. "They had a falling out sometime during the filming, which is why I replaced him as the voice of Pterri in the *Playhouse*'s second season. It may also be why he wasn't asked to write the second season of the show."

GOING BACK TO THE PLAYHOUSE

Before Reubens could dedicate himself wholeheartedly to *Big Top Pee-wee*, he had to deliver the *Playhouse*'s second season he had agreed to. The show was a hit, attracting younger viewers to the once geriatric CBS network, but there were a number of communication problems between Broadcast Arts and Reubens' team that needed to be addressed before production could continue.

"The first season was a roller-coaster ride," says Judy Price. "It was produced by this little outfit in New York. I wasn't totally comfortable with them, but they had a real imaginative group."

Price recalls one particular argument from early in the production process that exemplified the relationship between the two camps. Reubens wanted the playhouse door to be red and padded, as a visual reference to old diner booths. However, the team at Broadcast Arts installed the door in a different color because the material was more expensive in red. Ultimately, Reubens held his ground and his jagged red door became iconic.

"Paul had a very definite vision for everything," Price says. "He was involved in every aspect of that show. He would engage with the writing and art direction. Some would say he was difficult to work with, but he wasn't really. If you listened to him and helped him see his vision through, he was a happy camper."

"The proof's in the pudding," Richard Abramson adds. "The show was unbelievable and is still successful. Was Paul easy to work with? No. Was he right about most things? Absolutely. Did he always handle himself in a completely professional and mature way? Not all the time, but that was the way he got his points across."

While Reubens' creative vision drove the television series, the team at Broadcast Arts also saw themselves as bringing a unique set of talents to the table.

"At Broadcast Arts, we weren't just taking the Pee-wee franchise and mass producing it. We had our roots in mixed-media and the renaissance of stop-motion animation," says cofounder Steve Oakes. "We had the ability to do green screen and puppets from an artists' perspective. The show had a real New York aesthetic. We respected the audience of youngsters, but spoke to an MTV, teenage audience as well."

With Reubens' perfectionism and Broadcast Arts' inexperience in producing a television show of *Playhouse*'s magnitude, it wasn't long before tempers flared.

"Paul was sort of serving his time in New York and that made for some tension," Oakes says. "He is an artist that was very much hands-on with the approval of all the minutia of the show. He really delved into the details and ended up making the show great, but it was a chokepoint for expediting production."

Steve Oakes

Delays on the set were not only caused by Reubens' approval process, but also by the erratic mood swings of Reubens' manager and the executive producer of *Playhouse*, Richard Abramson.

"I'll be polite and say Rich was difficult," Oakes says. "He would throw these tantrums. He even put his fist through a wall one day and broke a bunch of bones in his hand and had to have his hand in a cast for most of the second half of the first season. I would guess, from his point of view he was doing the right thing for Paul, but he was not conducive to a fun working relationship. Paul was in a good cop/bad cop relationship with Rich. Paul was the funny guy that delivered the laughs and Rich was controlling and demanding. He didn't really have much empathy for what the process involved."

"I always tried to be reasonable," Abramson says. "But at the end of the day, it was my job to support Paul."

The on-set scuffles often led to phone calls to Judy Price and Michael Chase Walker at CBS, who would drop what they were doing in order to check on the production.

"I went out there several times because of problems," Price says. "There were lots of fires to put out."

It got worse: disagreements over creative decisions quickly gave way to problems over finances. According to Abramson, Broadcast Arts had agreed to pay for all expenses involved with producing the show before production began. Abramson and Reubens would handle their own salaries and they'd handle the music, for which composers would be paid a flat fee of $5,000 per episode. In principle, this arrangement had long-term benefits for Broadcast Arts, but in practice caused severe short-term pain.

"As the scripts were written, [Broadcast Arts] realized this was an expensive proposition and they weren't going to make a lot of money," Abramson says. "But in the beginning, it was the deal they wanted and the one they made."

"We were much too ambitious for our budget and that caused tension," Oakes says.

According to Oakes, Abramson would often request changes be made to the animation and that sequences be reshot. These demands caused the first season episodes to frequently run over budget and be delivered late to the network.

© John Duke Kisch / CBS

Richard Abramson and Greg Harrison

"Sometimes we wouldn't get a show delivered to CBS until Friday night," Price recalls. "I freaked out every week. It was like I was looking at this great abyss, wondering if this was going to be the week I would jump."

"There were all these demands made to change things and shoot beyond our schedule," Oakes says. "So we put a price tag on it and said, 'If you really want to shoot these extra days, this is what it's going to cost.' Rich wasn't very accommodating on any of those fronts, so we ended up in a lawsuit."

At the end of 1986, while *Playhouse* was just beginning to pick up steam in the ratings, Broadcast Arts sued Reubens for $900,000, which they said represented their share of the overages and the other monies owed.

"Paul and his managers, in the dispute about the overages, were withholding our payment," Oakes explains. "Not only withholding the overages, which we thought were fair for them to contribute to because they caused the overruns, but they weren't even paying the base amount that was in our contract, even though we delivered the show."

The cocktail of unbearably hot New York weather, inadequate shooting conditions, and distance from Reubens' homebase on the west coast, were enough reason for the star to want to move the production to Los Angeles for the second season.

"They told us they were taking the show to L.A. and asked us to send over all the props and puppets," Oakes recalls. "We said, 'Okay, send us our payment. What's it going to be?' Of course, they didn't, so the puppets stayed in storage until we got paid . . . and we didn't get paid for a long time."

Ultimately, the two parties reached an agreement and Broadcast Arts accepted a small settlement for the overages. After a few more attempts to come up with a hit television show, Broadcast Arts went bankrupt and dissolved in the early 1990s.

"*Pee-wee's Playhouse* was our first TV show at Broadcast Arts," Oakes recalls. "We aspired to evolve from doing commercials to long-form entertainment. One of the reasons why we were willing to go out on a limb financially was because we assumed that we'd make it up in toys and on the backend. We invested so much of our creative efforts and financial wherewithal that we thought we deserved to continue with the show."

"We never agreed to pay for overages," Abramson maintains. "Our deal didn't say we would pay for overages. It cost them more to do the show than they counted on, that's the bottom line, but maybe that's because they weren't efficient enough. The deal was very clear and concise, which is why they didn't get very much money from their lawsuit."

REBUILDING

Globey's look changed between the first and second seasons

With Broadcast Arts withholding the show's sets and puppets until payment was received, Reubens was left with the substantial problem of having to recreate the entire show from scratch. Gary Panter, along with Ric Heitzman and Wayne White, quickly redesigned a new set, taking advantage of the extra space afforded by the show's new soundstage at Hollywood Center Studios. White also redesigned the puppets, using his original sketches as references.

As many fans have noticed, the show's look dramatically changed between its first two seasons. The salesman and mutant toys were completely eliminated from the show. Most of the puppets received a facelift, with dramatic changes made to Globey in particular. His face remained in the same position — in the middle of the Atlantic Ocean — but the shape of his eyes changed, the brows increased mobility, and his nose went from thin and long to large and bulbous.

Puppet builders Marc Tyler and Steve Sleap were contracted by White to upgrade and remake a number of the puppets for the show's second season. They were assigned to work on the Cowntess costume, replacing its eye mechanism with remote controls and making her body and hindquarters look fuller.

Besides the additions made to the Cowntess's body, the functionality of the puppet remained unchanged. "Cowntess was a big, giant costume that I would stand inside during the New York shoot," George McGrath recalls. "There were two wooden sticks inside that moved the eyes and eyelashes. The mouth was a very heavy plastic that I would move with my hands. It was a very hot costume."

"They didn't really need too much done to the puppet," Tyler says. "All they really wanted was more cow."

As easy as it was to tweak the Cowntess, it was difficult to bring Randy back to the playhouse for the second season. The puppet used during the show's first season was carved from large blocks of white pine, which meant that Randy was unnecessarily heavy and difficult to manage. Before the second season, White asked Tyler and Sleap to redesign the puppet from his original drawings, but he asked them to carve the puppet out of basswood, a lighter material, and make his head out of fiberglass, which enabled the puppet builders to insert mechanisms that might allow for eyebrow movement. Puppet operator Van Snowden, who was best known for being the actor inside of H.R. Pufnstuf and had recently signed on to work on *Playhouse*, was instrumental in suggesting changes that were taken into Randy's redesign.

"He wanted to be able to pull a string to open the mouth instead of lowering a string," Tyler recalls. "So we had to mechanically reverse the action on that."

George McGrath and the Cowntess

Van Snowden

Despite the changes, Tyler believes the redone puppet was a suitable replacement for White's original.

"He was a perfect replica," Tyler recalls. "I think we fooled most people."

In addition to working on two established characters, Tyler and Sleap worked on Billy Baloney, a new *Playhouse* character introduced in the show's second season.

Billy's pint-sized stature was supposed to be much larger, according to Tyler. Wayne

© Ken Sax

Billy Baloney and Pee-wee

White's original sketches had him coming in at 26 inches and the builders abided by those sketches. However, when the puppet was sent to Paul Reubens for final approval, White came back with news that Reubens wanted it smaller. Despite the quick turnaround time required for the rebuild, Tyler believes Reubens' vision was correct.

"It stopped being a typical puppet when Wayne said to make him a little guy," Tyler says. "I think it was a very cool decision."

Knowing exactly how the puppet would be used on the show influenced the kinds of materials Tyler and Sleap used in its construction.

"We knew he was supposed to be a ventriloquist dummy," Tyler recalls. "He wasn't supposed to be a living character like Pterri or Randy. He was supposed to be a puppet."

As a result, Billy was made almost entirely out of polyethylene L200 foam. His head was covered with a thin layer of fiberglass, which enabled certain mechanisms to be mounted inside that could control his eye movements. Lynette Johnson, a miniature-clothing specialist, made his slacks and suit jacket.

For Tyler, one of the most rewarding aspects of his work on *Pee-wee's Playhouse* was seeing Billy turned into a toy.

"Oh, I geeked out about it," Tyler recalls. "I have one. The size and shapes are very close to the original. It probably works better than the one I had thrown together, frankly."

With the emergency puppet building already underway, the artistic team could turn their sights toward renovating and expanding the playhouse set. A multicolored wall was added that encased Pee-wee's toys, and the crew installed a renovated kitchen with a built-in booth that matched the playhouse door.

"If you have to make changes, why not make things better?" asks Prudence Fenton, the animation and effects supervisor.

With the larger space, Reubens added two characters in Puppetland: Clocky and Floory. Clocky returned from the original live show. Kevin Carlson gave the character life through movement and voice. Carlson was a big fan of Edie McClurg's performance in the

© Ken Sax

original production, but he was instrumental in reinventing the character's voice for the television show.

"When I first saw the character on the set and saw his wooden blocks with numbers painted on them that served as his teeth, I mentioned to Paul that they reminded me of braces," Carlson remembers. "So I sort of lisped his dialogue. Paul liked it and agreed that I should do the voice that way."

Clocky was built from a large slab of foam. Cuts were carved into the puppet to create a textured look, and the puppet was then painted yellow with erratic red grid marks. The mouth's mechanism was similar to that of a hand puppet, with a space provided where Carlson could spin the teeth-blocks as the character spoke. Large dowels were used to make Clocky's sides undulate.

Floory was another new character introduced in the show's second season. Carlson, who also provided the character's voice, liked the dichotomy between Floory's off-putting looks and the way he was treated by the other characters on the show.

"I just loved the fact that Floory wasn't a monster even though he was sort of scary look-ing and he even sounded kind of scary," he remembers. "Pee-wee just went towards him and said, 'Well, I guess I've got a new friend.' That was just very funny and nice to me."

With the move to L.A., Reubens dropped the five-person writing team and asked George McGrath to cowrite exclusively with him. Although McGrath and Reubens wrote the majority of the second season's scripts without any additional help, Reubens gave his friend Max Robert cowriting credit on all of the second season episodes so he would continue to stay on the payroll. "Max was very ill at the time," McGrath explains. "Paul, in one of the nicest gestures I've ever seen him make, kept him on staff although Max lived in San Francisco and only came down to work on scripts with us maybe two or three times."

The move also opened the door to casting changes. Mrs. Steve was written out, and Suzanne Kent, relieved of her duties working on *It's Garry Shandling's Show*, was able to join the *Playhouse* cast as Mrs. Rene, Pee-wee's high-energy next-door neighbor.

Mrs. Rene was based on a character Kent had created at the Groundlings named Rita Chandelier, a chatty Hollywood agent. The character grew out of an exercise in one of Groundlings' founder Gary Austin's classes.

"Gary would find something that he thought was funny and he would give you exercises to expand on it," Kent remem-

Suzanne Kent as Rita Chandelier with Groundling Joan Leizman

bers. "We did an exercise once to act as a relative that was close to you in your family, so I did my aunt. Part of my aunt, part of the women in my family, the New York Jewesses, and so that's how she came to be."

Rita Chandelier had had a trajectory similar to Pee-wee's. The character appeared on stage in several Groundlings shows and had even had a cameo in *Cheech and Chong's Nice Dreams*, but with one notable change: the filmmakers changed the character's name to Sidney the Agent. There are virtually no differences between Rita Chandelier and Sidney the Agent, but Kent made significant modifications when creating Mrs. Rene.

"The character was similar, except Rita Chandelier's main focal point was show business and her clients," Kent explains. "Whereas Mrs. Rene's main focal point was having fun and being flamboyant and being a shopper at all of the antique stores."

Because she had worked previously with many of the cast at the Groundlings, the actress had an easy job of assimilating into the group of *Playhouse* veterans.

© Ken Sax

"Everyone was just excited, and it was fun and colorful. It was like a big playground," Kent recalls. "We all worked really hard. We worked long hours and we enjoyed each other's company, so that made it better. I was familiar with the voices behind the puppets because I had known most of the people through the Groundlings, so that made me all the warmer toward the puppets."

As with the majority of the cast, Kent's background as an improvisational actor helped her to create Mrs. Rene's sense of style and love of fun. Although viewers at home never got to see inside the character's house, Kent knew exactly what the Rene household looked like, down to the home décor.

"Her house is filled with tchotchkes and all kinds of fabrics and glass bottles and vases and flowers," Kent says. "You know, oriental rugs and hanging lamps. Not one space that's empty. Everything's filled with something. But neat, not dirty. Clean, but filled with lots of things. I also visualize Mrs. Rene having many little dogs, and playing mah-jongg, and just kind of being the social Jewish maiden in the neighborhood."

Gilbert Lewis did not reprise his role as the King of Cartoons; instead, the part went to William Marshall of *Blacula* fame. Vic Trevino was brought on to play Ricardo, a new character written for the show's second season to replace Tito the Lifeguard, who was played by Roland Rodriguez during the show's first season. The role of Dixie, the King's cabbie, was written out.

© John Duke Kisch / CBS

Shaun Weiss, Natasha Lyonne, and Diane Yang

"I wasn't offered to go to Los Angeles," Johann Carlo says. "It would have been nice to do, but it was what it was. If I was asked, I would have done it. I liked Paul and liked doing the show."

Natasha Lyonne (who would later go on to critical acclaim in 1998's *Slums of Beverly Hills*), Shaun Weiss, and Diane Yang were replaced as the Playhouse Gang. Vaughn Tyree Jelks, Alisan Porter (who went on to star as the title character in 1991's *Curly Sue*), and Stephanie Walski all took to their new roles with ease and enthusiasm.

"It was a really great experience," Walski says. "Paul was extremely kind to all the parents and children [on the set]. It was a really fun environment to work in. My birthday was on one of our shooting days and the whole crew had a party for me. They were all really kind."

Because she had been familiar with the show from its first season, Walski remembers being particularly excited about her audition.

"It was really fun," she says. "I was definitely a very outgoing child. During my final callback Paul was there and he asked me if I could sing a cappella. At the time I didn't know what that meant, so I said, 'No, but I can sing 'You're Never Fully Dressed Without a Smile!' I thought a cappella was a song or something. I sang for him and showed him how I could do the Pee-wee dance. He thought it was all really funny."

With Paragon stripped of his role as the voice of Pterri, his only involvement in the show was appearing as Jambi. Despite the changing of the guard, Paragon took the modification with maturity and grace.

"It made things a little awkward when John was on the set," McGrath recalls. "However, knowing Paul as well as he did, John completely understood that replacing him wasn't my doing. He made that clear before the season began shooting. I spoke to him about it before-hand because I didn't want him to get the idea that I had lobbied for the part. He was actually really cool about it. At least he was to my face."

Greg Harrison, who had provided the movement for Conky during the show's first season, was replaced by Kevin Carlson. According to Carlson, his casting was due in large part to his ability to fit inside the puppet's small body. Despite the confining nature of performing inside a four-foot-tall puppet, Carlson enjoyed the opportunity to play Conky.

"It was actually quite great being inside the puppet because Conky was pretty much front and center in the playhouse," Carlson remembers. "The helmet part of the costume had a glass window where I could see out but people couldn't see me looking at them. A lot of times I was just taking in the whole process of shooting the show."

With the set and puppets now being reconstructed and a new cast in place, production continued on *Pee-wee's Playhouse*. However, as the train started to leave the station, Reubens remembered he was still without a conductor. With Broadcast Arts no longer producing the show, Reubens asked his friend Steve Binder, a television producer and director, if he had any

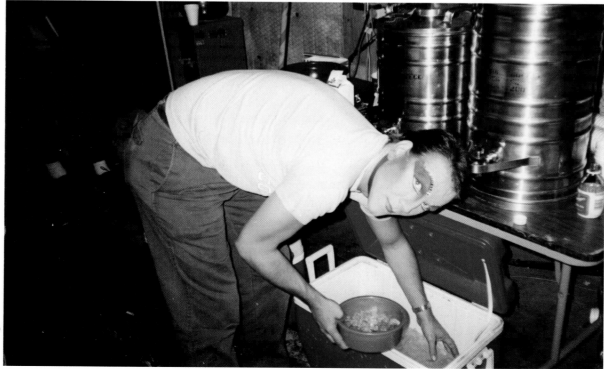

© George McGrath

© Ken Sax

© John Duke Kisch / CBS

Sid Bartholomew

suggestions for who might be suitable to executive produce the next two seasons of the show.

"I met him at his office at Paramount," Binder recalls. "We spoke a little while and he asked if I would be interested in producing it. I hadn't even thought of it at all. I asked what that would entail and he said that we would go in as partners. He would own it, but my production company would produce it."

Binder initially thought Reubens' proposal was a joke, but he gave it serious consideration. Within hours he had decided to accept the offer.

"I always enjoyed working with young people and Paul seemed to have put together an interesting group of professionals and nonprofessionals," Binder says. "I enjoyed watching his New York season. I thought it was excellent."

The onslaught of positive reviews and high ratings for the show's first season cast a daunting shadow as production forged ahead.

"My first major task was to be as good as the New York season," Binder recalls. "I have no critique of what they did. In fact, I knew that when people watched season two they would compare it to season one. I think we had some pretty good results. I don't remember getting any critiques from Judy Price or the network. Paul came to work every day with a smile on his face, along with the rest of the crew, and I think it was a pretty smooth operation."

While most of the season flowed a lot more easily than the tumultuous first season, it started with an expensive and nearly fatal series of complications. Stephen R. Johnson, the director from the show's first season, was rehired to continue working in Los Angeles. Nearly immediately, his working style caused him to butt heads with Binder.

"I broke down the script for the first episode with the staff and asked Steve who he wanted to do the storyboards," Binder explains. "He told me he didn't use storyboard artists. I asked him how he directed his music videos if he didn't use storyboards and he said, 'I kind of wing them and get inspired on the set.' I told him that I was a great believer in preproduction and homework. We couldn't afford to waste time with his thinking creatively."

Binder hired a storyboard artist to draft the first episode, but to his surprise, Johnson refused to meet with him. After a follow-up conversation during which Johnson became belligerent, Binder let the director go. With Johnson gone, Binder promoted the assistant director, giving him the responsibility of shooting the first episode of the season.

The new director wanted to use a new device called a barber crane, which would give the camera more mobility. However, the technology was relatively new and the crane was particularly sensitive and hard to operate. When the son of the crane's inventor signed on to operate the machinery, Binder agreed to use it.

However, problems soon arose when it came time to get the film processed. Reubens insisted on shooting the show on film, as opposed to videotape, in order to achieve a more cinematic look for the episodes. However, because 16mm film was becoming an antiquated way of shooting, the lab processing the film had to use equally antiquated methods, which made for significant delays in providing the crew with dailies. As a result, no footage was screened until the entire first episode was shot. When the footage came back, Binder remembers being horrified by what he saw.

"The show was a disaster," he recalls. "The camera was bouncing all over the place and it looked unprofessional. I had just spent about four hundred thousand dollars on this show and I couldn't let it air. I knew that if people saw the episode it would be the end of *Pee-wee's Playhouse*."

Without giving it a second thought, Binder made the decision to cut his losses and scrap the episode. He fired the newly promoted assistant director and asked his friend Guy Louthan to fill in.

"I went to Paul and told him instead of shooting the second show, we were going to shoot the first show again and throw away the negatives on the one we shot," Binder recalls. "Paul was blown away. He couldn't believe that I would make that decision."

© Ken Sax

Although the reshoot put the production behind schedule, Binder was pleased with the results.

"We restarted with a whole new crew and got rid of that unreliable piece of equipment," he says. "Eight hundred thousand dollars later, the first episode went off without a hitch. I think the decision saved the *Playhouse*. If I aired it we would have been crucified."

After filming the episode, Reubens expressed interest in directing. Although Paul was enthusiastic, Binder harbored doubts about the actor's ability to steer the ship in the right direction by himself. As a compromise, Binder hired Wayne Orr, a gifted cameraman, to codirect with Reubens.

"I felt Paul needed someone who really understood structure," Binder explains.

"Without a doubt, Wayne was the best cameramen in electronic media."

The two met to discuss their vision for the show's second season. Orr and Reubens hit it off right away, and this made for a seamless working relationship.

"Paul has a great talent for communicating with people," Orr says. "It works when he speaks directly to his viewers and I thought it could be fun to take that to the next level, so we had a lot of shots of Paul speaking directly to the camera. It allowed him to perform without doing a lot of cutting. When I first discussed the show with him, Paul told me he didn't want to see a lot of cutting, even though it had been fashionable at the time with music videos. He wanted to have time for kids to see something and absorb it, and I totally got that."

Wayne Orr agreed to work on *Playhouse*, but only on a limited basis.

"My agreement with them was that I would do it for a week and then I would let them know if I wanted to stay on," Orr explains. "If they didn't want me, they could say, 'Thank you very much, we enjoyed having you here, but we're going in another direction.' I knew going into it that there was a certain tension because they were a week behind schedule, so I wanted to be able to bow out gracefully if need be."

At the end of his third day, Orr had gotten the show back on schedule. Binder told him that he was welcome to stay and codirect the remainder of the season with Reubens if he wanted and Orr accepted.

REANIMATION

With Broadcast Arts out of the picture, Reubens' biggest hurdle was finding a team of artists to animate the stop-motion sequences. Prudence Fenton left Broadcast Arts to retain her role as animation and effects producer on *Playhouse*, but few others who had worked on the first season made the move west. Fenton's first order of business was to assemble a team that could not only work at a brisk pace, but also retain the look and integrity of the inaugural episodes.

Craig Bartlett, who later went on to create the Nickelodeon channel's series *Hey Arnold*, was hired to animate the Penny cartoons. For him the experience was stress-free, despite a rigorous shooting schedule.

"We had ten weeks to shoot ten shorts," Bartlett remembers. "That meant a couple weeks of story-editing the recordings and drawing storyboards, then a week or so of building, then shooting each one-minute Penny cartoon in three or four days."

Unlike the tumultuous job of getting approval for the show's opening sequence for the first season, Bartlett found the approval process to be easy.

"We edited our pieces from the interviews with the girls into one-minute tapes, and then drew simple storyboards," he says. "We went to Hollywood to meet with Paul every couple weeks to show him a couple storyboards and he would either say yes or no to them. If the answer was no, I had to just start over with a new idea. It was that simple. Once the sequences were shot, there were no changes at all."

Don Waller took over for Kent Burton animating the dinosaur sequences, while Tom McLaughlin took over the ant farm. The refrigerator sequences were animated by Doug Chiang.

While the established animated sequences continued to earn adulation in the show's second season, the most memorable segments were two sections from the "School" episode. In that installment, Pee-wee and Magic Screen explain Christopher Columbus's discovery of America and the signing of the Declaration of Independence in two clips animated by Dave Daniels. What makes these sequences stand out is the unique strata-cut animation style that has remained impossible to duplicate, even to this day.

To animate with a strata-cut technique, Daniels built an entire sequence into an oblong-shaped clay loaf. He would then cut the loaf into 1/8-inch slices to reveal the animation inside. The result was a sequence that seemed less like traditional stop-motion and more like computer animation.

"Viewing it as a two-dimensional animation on screen is a little weaker than when you are in the presence of the actual loaf," Daniels says. "By the time I was doing this in the mid-'90s, people assumed it was being done with a computer. People in the presence of it see a real performance piece and understand the planning that went into it."

Daniels' achievements with strata-cut made him one of the most respected of the *Playhouse* animators. He is the only person to have animated on all of the show's seasons. After *Playhouse*, he opened his own animation studio and is responsible for designing and animating the talking M&Ms commercials.

Animators Craig Bartlett and Dave Daniels

© Dave Daniels

BRANDING THE PLAYHOUSE

Karen Lyons' early prototype of the Pterri doll

In addition to his other responsibilities on set, Reubens frequently took meetings with companies offering to collaborate on officially licensed Pee-wee Herman merchandise. Matchbox toys, best known for Hot Wheels, their die-cast miniature car line, signed on to release an extensive catalog of *Pee-wee's Playhouse* merchandise. Karen Lyons, one of the designers on the Matchbox plush toy line, remembers her process of creating the toys for Pterri and Chairry.

"I had been working as a freelance designer for several companies and became known as the designer who could handle the weird and unusual designs," she explains. "Beth Hall of Matchbox toys contacted me and asked if I would like to tackle the Pee-wee Herman line they were working on. Of course, I jumped at the chance. I already was a fan and thought *Pee-wee's Playhouse* was the most creative show around at the time."

While the offer was exciting, the task of creating plush toys with elaborate mechanisms inside them was daunting.

"This was the first time that soft toys would have so much interaction with the owner," Lyons says. "Paul wanted toys that were original. Chairry had to talk and roll her eyes and Pterri had to have wings that flapped and eyes that moved. It was a challenge. Some of the solid toy designers had complicated mechanisms they suggested, but these designs couldn't work with soft designs because the stuffing exerts a lot of pressure on any mechanism and there were no fixed points to attach supports. It really pushed me as a designer and I loved it. At the end of the day, the toys were well received by the public and Paul Reubens' ideas were proven worth the extra design work."

While the process of designing Pterri and Chairry was challenging, the biggest challenge lay in creating the 18-inch talking Pee-wee Herman doll. From the concept's inception, Reubens was insistent that the doll be built with a pull-string mechanism, an antiquated style of building talking toys.

"He insisted upon the doll not being battery operated," Judy Price recalls. "He wanted it to be usable by all children. Pull-string toys don't require batteries."

Reubens ultimately won the pull-string battle, and the results were good but short lived.

Though many dolls are still in existence, few have maintained the power of speech. The most common complaint about the doll in later years is that it speaks too fast. Recognizing the limitations of the technology, Matchbox rereleased the doll in 2000, and this time, Pee-wee's voice was activated by pressing his stomach.

The process of approving the doll was difficult, especially when it came to sculpting a head that closely resembled Pee-wee's.

"I can't tell you how many heads we went through," Reubens says. "It just didn't look like me. It was always supposed to be a cartoon — it wasn't supposed to be me. That was a decision we made pretty early on. But the doll just didn't look right."

Ultimately the doll was completed and, much to Reubens' delight, it was an immediate hit with children.

© Ken Sax

Pee-wee with his doll on the *Playhouse* set

"I don't know exactly how many dolls were sold," Reubens says. "But I have one they gave me in a case honoring the one-millionth doll sold."

In addition to the plush toys, Matchbox also released six-inch poseable action figures in the likeness of many *Playhouse* characters. Characters like Pterri, Conky, and Magic Screen were given movement with a wind-up mechanism, which, like the Pee-wee doll's pull-string device, gave the toys a distinctly retro feel. The figurines fit perfectly inside the most elaborate piece of *Playhouse* merchandise, a deluxe playset crafted in the image of the television show's set. Although the majority of the *Playhouse* characters were sold separately, the set did have its own unique features such as a working front door, hands that spin on Clocky, and a moveable Floory. The toy was so accurate that when John Paragon and Paul Reubens codirected the show in the fourth and fifth seasons, they used the playset to block the action.

Later, a Billy Baloney ventriloquist doll and Vance the Talking Pig, from *Big Top Pee-wee*, were also released as soft-body dolls.

Pee-wee's Playhouse merchandise was not limited to toys. During the show's run, JC Penney exclusively carried a line of Pee-wee Herman clothing, including blue jeans, sweaters, and T-shirts. A.C. Reed released a brand of Pee-wee party products; Collegeville put out an officially licensed Pee-wee Herman Halloween costume; and Topps released a line of collectible trading cards, just to name a few. Throughout the '80s it was virtually impossible to escape Pee-wee Herman memorabilia.

In an understatement, George McGrath says, "Paul had the merchandising opportunities covered pretty well."

Perhaps the rarest collectible items are a full-sized Chairry, put out by Foam Merchants, and a 48-inch non-talking Pee-wee Herman doll. These items occasionally turn up on eBay, fetching several hundred dollars each.

While there was no shortage of Pee-wee merchandise released in the mid- to late '80s, several items got stalled in development. In 1987, toy designer Timothy Young worked on a prototype for a talking Penny doll that was to be released by Matchbox alongside the Pterri and Chairry dolls. However, the project was killed before Penny could hit store shelves.

"The doll was never produced," Young recalls, "because the marketing department at Matchbox felt that since she didn't interact with any of the other Pee-wee characters, she was not viable as a toy."

PENNY
15" TALKING DOLL

© Timothy Young

Timothy Young's design and prototype for the unreleased Penny doll

Young's prototype was an 18-inch doll, crafted similarly to the talking Pee-wee Herman. The head was made of a thick plastic, attached to a bendable plush body wearing Penny's signature blue dress. If released, Penny would have said several phrases and presumably would have been pull-string operated.

Reubens had other ideas that stalled before reaching the prototyping phase. One was a line of Miss Yvonne wigs and makeup; another was that he would market colognes (Pee-wee Number Five and Eau de Pee-wee), but Reubens had a hard time drumming up interest in them.

"Nobody wanted to do the wigs," he says. "I thought it would have been really funny for little girls to be going to school with these huge wigs on."

One other unreleased project very nearly made it to stores: Purina brand Pee-wee Chow, breakfast cereal intended for kids to eat on their hands and knees. The cereal made it all the way to a blind taste test — kids overwhelmingly hated it.

"The company wanted to go back to the drawing board, but it would have been so time consuming that I didn't want to do it," Reubens says.

Although some projects didn't materialize, there was enough merchandising to keep Reubens busy when he wasn't on the set. At a time when children's television was under fire for being too merchandise-driven, Judy Price was relieved to see that Reubens' approach was free of criticism from parent advocacy groups.

"*Pee-wee's Playhouse* was more the exception than the rule in regards to merchandising," she says. "In the 1980s, a lot of shows were actually based on toys. The toy came first and then the show. There was no merchandising out during the *Playhouse*'s first year. Paul missed the bandwagon partially because he was too much of a perfectionist. He didn't want the merchandise to wag the dog. He wanted to do a show, and do a good show, and then the merchandising would follow."

Fan Dennis Manochio with his collection of Pee-wee memorabilia

BACK TO THE CIRCUS

Unlike the show's first awkward year, the second season shoot was relatively smooth sailing. The shows came in on time and within budget.

"It's a matter of personal pride for me that we weren't wasting a lot of time," says Wayne Orr. "I got two hundred pages of storyboards and they gave me the idea of what to do. I was very confident while I was shooting that everything would work, and it did."

In addition to the rigorous workload of writing, producing, starring in, and codirecting episodes, Reubens also made time to meet with terminally ill children whose dying wish was to meet Pee-wee Herman.

Pee-wee takes a break to visit a young fan

© John Duke Kisch / CBS

"Paul always had time for kids," Orr says. "He was nice to everybody, but to kids he was an absolutely nice host. He would be Pee-wee most of the time, a very calm Pee-wee, and would show them around the set. He deserves real kudos for that."

The second season of *Pee-wee's Playhouse* was an overwhelming success. The show finished first in its timeslot, cementing its position as the dominating children's television program on Saturday morning. That year, the show was nominated for 13 Emmy Awards, more than any other children's television show has ever been nominated for in one year, with the exception of *Sesame Street*. The show took home three awards, for Outstanding Art Direction/Set Direction/Scenic Design, Outstanding Achievement in Makeup, and Outstanding Achievement in Videotape Editing.

While working on the show's second season, Reubens and McGrath continued working on *Big Top Pee-wee*.

"We really started from scratch, screening a lot of circus movies on the Paramount lot, and kicking ideas around before we pitched it to the head of Paramount," McGrath recalls. "The pre-writing period was longer than the writing."

The head of Paramount green-lit the picture and signed *Grease* director Randal Kleiser as director, and preproduction officially began. Although Kleiser was enthusiastic about the project, his sensibilities might not have been a perfect fit for a Pee-wee film.

"Randal is a nice guy and he's pretty talented," says Richard Abramson, who was an executive producer on the film. "But he's not Tim Burton. He just really wanted to work on the project and campaigned until he got it."

The process of working on both a hit television show and a major motion picture may have stretched Reubens too far.

"It was really annoying when he was working on the movie because he definitely was distracted by the movie," Prudence Fenton recalls. "The movie seemed to be cooler and more glamorous than a little TV show, but he worked it out."

Paul Reubens taking a break from working on the *Big Top Pee-wee* script in Hawaii

Reubens and McGrath headed to Hawaii to write the script at Kleiser's home. While the duo worked excellently together, McGrath harbored concerns about some of Reubens' choices.

"The only thing that Paul definitely wanted to be in the script had very little to do with the circus," McGrath recalls. "He wanted the longest screen kiss in movie history. I think he wanted it to be the answer to a trivia question."

Even before the film's release, an extended kiss, shared with the 21-year-old actress Valeria Golino in her first American film, confused critics and polarized the public. Decades after the film's release, it remains impossible to mention *Big Top Pee-wee* without talking about the kiss heard 'round the world.

"This kiss, unbelievable," Golino told the *Los Angeles Times* in a 1988 interview. "To me, it's one of my favorite scenes because it goes on so long that it will for sure get a reaction out of the public."

That proved to be a gross understatement. Paramount began publicizing the kiss as a three-minute-sixteen-second epic a month before the film's release, declaring that it was going to unseat the lip-lock between Jane Wyman and Regis Tommey in the 1941 film *You're in the Army Now*, which clocked in at three minutes, five seconds. Curiously, the kiss was edited down to less than two minutes long and never achieved the milestone that Reubens sought.

Courtesy Paramount Pictures / PhotoFest © Paramount Pictures

Gina (Valeria Golino) and Pee-wee Herman

In the run-up to the film's release, Reubens talked up the movie's romantic subplots.

"I've got an active libido in the new picture," Reubens said, in character. "In *Big Adventure* I was obsessed with an object. In *Big Top*, I'm obsessed with love."

Of course, for a character who famously described himself as a loner and rebel, an obsession with love struck many as an ill-conceived character choice.

"It was a big misjudgment, as far as I was concerned," McGrath recalls.

"When you're working on a movie, it's always great while you're working on it," explains Scott Chester, who was an associate producer on the film as well as Paul's personal assistant. "I was so involved on day-to-day production that when we were doing the circus scenes and watching the hippo chase a pig down the hill, it looked like it had all those great Pee-wee elements. However, there was a point when I was watching him fall in love and having that long kiss and I just stopped in my tracks out of confusion."

Critics and audiences cited the film as evidence that Reubens was attempting to mature the Pee-wee Herman character, an observation McGrath disagrees with.

"I'm not sure it was decided that Pee-wee would grow up," McGrath says. "I don't think

Pee-wee with Winnie (Penelope Ann Miller) in *Big Top Pee-wee*

he was really grown up. In *Big Adventure* he was dealing with Dottie, but this movie just took it a little further. I never really thought of his 'growing up' being a step the movie took, and I'm pretty sure Paul didn't either."

While McGrath's statement has merit, it ignores significant differences between Pee-wee's relationships in the two films. In *Big Adventure*, Pee-wee has an obvious aversion to a romantic relationship with Dottie, the tomboy played by E.G. Daily, who works at the shop that services his bike. Despite her repeated attempts to get him to like her, he puts on a faux machismo act and ignores her advances. By the end of the movie, the duo has some sort of strengthened relationship, but it is left ambiguous as to whether or not their connection is romantic.

However, when *Big Top* starts, Pee-wee is engaged to schoolteacher Winnie, played by Penelope Ann Miller, with whom he publicly displays affection in front of kindergarteners. The character then falls in love with Gina, the Golino character, and has an affair. There is even a suggested sex scene with a montage of cinematic clichés including images of volcanoes erupting and a train entering a tunnel.

The true failure of the kiss isn't simply that its adulterous nature might have offended some parents, but that to the majority of children in the audience, the romantic elements were simply disinteresting at best, disgusting at worse. Most children cover their eyes or recoil when their parents share a moment of intimacy; Pee-wee Herman was someone they saw as their developmental equal.

Since the character's inception, Pee-wee Herman has always walked a tightrope balanced between man and child, generous and self-centered, masculine and feminine. Although he famously asked, "I know you are, but what am I," most people preferred the question to remain rhetorical.

Surprisingly, Reubens' view of the purpose of the kiss was similar to that of the critics. In fact, he has stated in interviews that he had intended to continue to mature the character. Although *Big Top Pee-wee* may have seemed to signal a new beginning in the character's cinematic career, perhaps the actor in the red bow tie saw it as the first step in an exit plan.

THE BEARDED LADY SINGS

Paramount launched a full-on publicity offensive for *Big Top Pee-wee* in the summer of 1988. Several press releases were sent out updating journalists on the film's progress, and Reubens was made available for in-character interviews to talk up the film's prospects. Despite the level of access granted to reporters, few seemed enthusiastic about Pee-wee Herman's latest adventure. Many wondered publicly how the character could survive a film with a romantic subplot, whether the film would repeat the box office success of *Adventure*, and how Pee-wee would function in a circus environment. Some reporters even expressed frustration with being forced to interview only Pee-wee Herman, while Reubens was allegedly "unavailable for comment."

"Entertainment writers are always informed that Pee-wee Herman will be interviewed as Pee-wee

Courtesy Paramount Pictures / PhotoFest © Paramount Pictures

Herman, the film and television star, not as Paul Reubens, his real-life identity," Associated Press reporter Bob Thomas wrote in a 1988 article. "How do you deal with that? Would you interview Lucille Ball as Lucy Ricardo? Sean Connery as James Bond? How to question Pee-wee Herman? In squeaks and baby talk?"

Despite the less-than-favorable advance press the film received, Reubens remained optimistic that *Big Top* would find an audience and repeat the success of his original film — that is, until the film's star-studded premiere. After the film rolled, and stars like Penelope Ann Miller and Kris Kristofferson started working the crowd, Reubens approached McGrath to talk.

"Paul sat down next to me and said, 'Well, you know the film is a bomb, right?'" McGrath remembers. "He explained that he could tell from the way people were talking to him at the party, not that anyone said anything bad about the film per se, but their remarks indicated they didn't like it as much as the first film."

Big Top Pee-wee hit theaters July 22, 1988, to heavy publicity and minimal box office returns. The film made $15.1 million at the domestic box office, just over a third of *Big Adventure*'s overall haul. It was an undeniable misstep.

"I wasn't pleased with the film," McGrath says. "Paul's insistence on having Italians cast in any role that had an Italian last name was a mistake; so much of what was funny in the script was barely understandable in their hands. But the worst miscasting was of the elderly townspeople. They were supposed to be Margaret Hamilton–type villains and could have been cast with younger character actresses like Suzanne Kent and Lynne Stewart. Instead, they cast a lot of very sympathetic-looking, really old women who always seemed to be victims. You ended up hating Pee-wee for being mean to them instead of vice versa."

According to associate producer Scott Chester, the casting was not the only facet of the film's production where Reubens was steadfast in seeing his vision through. The actor had unprecedented creative control, overseeing all aspects of the shoot.

"Paul had a lot more autonomy on the second film," Chester says. "It was different when we were at Warner Brothers and he hadn't made a film. They weren't yes-men on the first movie, let's put it that way."

"He's extraordinarily talented, but he's not great at everything," Richard Abramson says. "He's not great at managing people. He's great at playing the character, but when he has total control and there's no collaboration, he isn't at his best."

Judy Price believes the film's lackluster performance at the box office may have been due to Pee-wee's television success.

"The one thing I thought the movie did wrong was give Pee-wee an age," she says. "Children didn't see him as an adult. This is born out by research that was done way back in the early days of the television show. If you were eight years old, you viewed him as eight. In *Big Top Pee-wee*, he had romantic involvement and that aged him."

Richard Abramson agrees.

"Besides the fact that the second movie was a piece of shit, I think the success of the *Playhouse* made the second movie do as poorly as it did," he says. "For the first movie, Pee-wee's target audience was college kids. After having an enormously successful [children's] television show, it was harder for college kids to publicly support a character that their younger brothers and sisters were fond of. They might have watched privately in their dorm rooms, but that's a different thing from having to declare you're a Pee-wee fan at a ticket booth."

Although Reubens was devastated by the audience reaction to the film, there was no blowback from CBS — *Big Top*'s performance would not affect *Playhouse*.

"I was surprised the second movie didn't do as well as the first," Price recalls. "But there honestly was never a concern about it at the network. In fact, any movie release usually enhances the awareness of a character and/or property, even with a lackluster box office, especially with the additional promotion. Of course, a blockbuster movie is even better."

The commercial failure of *Big Top Pee-wee* caused Paramount to terminate the development deal, killing plans for a gangster film Reubens had hoped to work on next.

"Paul has always wanted to do a *Pee-wee Confidential* film," McGrath recalls. "He and I spoke about it several times. There would be '50s-style blaring horns and Pee-wee would be involved in the seedy side of the city. I think it would have been a funny movie."

Instead, Pee-wee returned to Saturday morning, putting Reubens' career goals of being a movie star on hold for a second time.

4 | A CHRISTMAS STORY

© Sarah Llewllyn

BY THE FALL OF 1988, *Pee-wee's Playhouse* was undeniably the most successful and well-thought-of children's show on television. Merchandise was flying off toy store shelves, Pee-wee Herman had become one of the most recognizable public figures in America, and colleges across the country were beginning to use the show as an instructional aid in art classes.

Although Reubens was eager to return to work, an unexpected roadblock met him at the playhouse door. The Writers Guild of America (WGA) had a strike, and production on the show's third season was delayed due to a lack of scripts. Ultimately, only two episodes were produced for the show's third season. Both were written by John Paragon, who had since reconciled his differences with Reubens and returned to being a pivotal member of the show's creative team.

With the Writers Guild strike paralyzing the show for most of its third season, network executives at CBS were determined to come up with a way to compensate for the loss, while also tapping into the show's adult fan base. Soon after Reubens' promotional tour for *Big Top Pee-wee*, CBS executives approached executive producer Steve Binder with an idea.

"CBS came to me and they said, 'We have such a huge college market for the show,'" Binder recalls. "'Do you think you can deliver a primetime special?' And so Paul and I decided we would go for it."

The network had been toying with the idea of putting the show on in prime time ever since its first season. A 1986 *Newsday* article cites sources at CBS as saying that the network was considering running *Playhouse* twice a week before *Late Night with David Letterman*. Richard Abramson lobbied in vain for *Playhouse* to be broadcast at a time more accessible to adults.

"I tried to convince CBS to run the show Friday night at midnight, but they didn't see the value in it," he explains. "I was trying to maintain some sort of connection with the college kid audience. Luckily, they ended up finding the show anyway, staying up all night drinking on Fridays and watching the show buzzed Saturday morning."

Binder also thought Pee-wee would work well in prime time and pitched Reubens a late-night television spin-off about the secret life of Miss Yvonne as a "kinky next-door neighbor" in Puppetland. While actress Lynne Stewart was enthused about the idea, Reubens was not.

Pee-wee and Santa meet for the first time in *Pee-wee's Big Adventure*

Even while promoting the Christmas special, Reubens publicly expressed doubt about whether the show would appeal to a broader audience in prime time.

"I think half the reason adults like the show is that they're semi-groggy when they watch it," Reubens said in character during a 1988 promotional interview. "Then again, the same rationale could apply to late night."

The strike ended on August 7, which didn't give the creative team a lot of time to prepare for a Christmas special that had yet to be written. Reubens was eager to get back to work after *Big Top*'s disappointing box office performance.

"The real story behind the Christmas special is the failure of *Big Top Pee-wee*," Reubens admitted in a 1997 interview. "[The movie] wasn't a smash hit, to say the least. I'd had no failure up to that point and I kind of got blocked [thanks to] that."

Motivated to prove the film's box office returns had no bearing on his creativity, Reubens and cowriter John Paragon let their imaginations run wild. A new animated opening sequence would be shot, with an opening number featuring the United States Marine Corps Choir. The show's runtime would be expanded to a full hour. Reubens also had another sure-fire way to drum up interest in the special.

"We were constantly being called by agents, managers, and stars themselves, wanting to get on the *Playhouse*," Binder recalls. "Paul insisted that the show just be our repertoire company. I think he made up for it with the number of guest stars in the Christmas special."

Reubens and Paragon hit the ground running. They wrote the episode in only five days in Reubens' office at Paramount Studios. Heeding criticism that *Big Top Pee-wee*'s plot was too far reaching, the two made sure their script focused on the festivities and fun of the holiday season.

"It's a little thin on story," Reubens said in character during a 1988 interview. "I didn't want to weigh it down with a lot of heavy thought."

Writing a conventional holiday special also made it easier to work within the time constraints.

"I remember one of the things that made this special write itself was the fact that there were kind of so many iconic things to Christmas," Reubens recalls. In an homage to past television specials, *Pee-wee's Playhouse Christmas Special* includes the characters drinking hot chocolate by a roaring fireplace, singing Christmas carols, reenacting the nativity scene that explains the true meaning of Christmas, and an angry little puppet screaming, "Bah, Humbug!"

DECKING THE PLAYHOUSE HALLS

As principal photography began on the special, the animators began working on their sequences. The most daunting task was recreating the show's "Happy Village" opening. The grazing deer and curious rabbits had to be replaced with mechanical elves and a curious fox scurrying over a blanket of snow. Guest animator Joel Fletcher, who had worked with animation and effects producer Prudence Fenton on previous non-*Playhouse* projects, was brought on to animate the opening sequence.

The new, winterized opening was shot on November 25, 1988, over 12 hours. However, in the middle of the night, a low-impact earthquake tremor caused the entire sequence to have to be reshot.

"In those days, once you started a stop-motion shoot you had to keep going until it was completely finished," Fletcher explains. "The shot was extremely long with an elaborate camera move which required animating until the wee hours of the morning. In order for the miniature Christmas lights to shine bright enough, the camera had to run through the move a second time with a special exposure for the lights. The earthquake caused a misalignment

© Joel Fletcher

on the second light pass and ruined the shot. I had to pull another all-nighter to reshoot the animation. The little fox I sculpted for the sequence had to be rebuilt as well since it was made of clay and was pretty beat up from animating the first shot. I'm pretty sure the first version was better, but we will never know."

Fletcher remembers Reubens visiting the animation stage to see how the reshoots were going. "Paul stopped by to see how the animation was coming along," he recalls. "I had never met him before. It was surreal to see him in costume and makeup, yet speaking with a normal voice. I think he had a pack of cigarettes in the top pocket of his outfit, which seemed out of context as well."

The reshoot was worth the time. Fenton and Fletcher were nominated for an Emmy Award in the category of Outstanding Achievement in Graphic Design and Title Sequences.

Pee-wee's Playhouse Christmas Special was nominated for Emmys in two additional categories. Gary Panter, Ric Heitzman, Wayne White, Jimmy Cuomo, Paul Reubens, and Deborah Madalena-Lloyd were nominated for Outstanding Art Direction for a Variety or Music Program. Max Robert and Robert Turturice were nominated for Outstanding Costume Design for a Variety or Music Program.

The evening of the Emmy Awards was bittersweet for the *Playhouse* crew. Although it was an honor to be nominated, they had been informed that not enough votes had been cast in the Graphic Design and Title Sequences category, which meant that there would be no winner. As a result, Prudence Fenton decided not to appear at the Emmys in protest. Fletcher attended with his girlfriend, as the only representative from the Christmas special nominees.

"Actually, without the anxiety of wondering who would win, it allowed us to fully enjoy the evening," Fletcher recalls.

Tuturice, who also designed the costumes for *Big Top Pee-wee*, created a memorable dress for Miss Yvonne on the Christmas special that caused a wardrobe malfunction long before Janet Jackson and Justin Timberlake at the Super Bowl. The lighting apparatus inside Lynne Stewart's wig short-circuited and began smoking, which in turn caused her red-and-green Christmas tree–inspired dress to spark and nearly catch fire while filming. Several cast and crew members went to her rescue, taking off her famous bouffant and removing the power pack that controlled the lights.

Stewart escaped unscathed and has fond memories of the costume, which she still has and wears publicly whenever possible.

"I've worn the dress to kids' parades and benefits," Stewart says. "When the kids were too young to know who Miss Yvonne was, I told them I was Santa's second wife, Jennifer Claus!"

Steven Perfidia Kirkham

Lynne Stewart in 2010 wearing her *Christmas Special* dress

Miss Yvonne wasn't the only *Playhouse* character to get into the Christmas spirit. The art directors and set designers worked overtime to transform the set into a winter wonderland. All of the puppets and human characters were decked out in scarves, mittens, and snow boots. The festive costumes and the completely redecorated playhouse set created a look that was uniquely Pee-wee but still classically Christmas. Some of the special additions included a new wing to the playhouse that appeared to be made entirely out of fruitcake and a Christmas tree made out of a barbeque grill and train set.

In a 1998 *Newsday* interview, Reubens recalled, "I got a lot of cool new stuff from the special. When the art department was packing things up they were missing quite a few things."

The animation department also put a holiday feel on their sequences. The Penny cartoon involved a quest for Christmas gifts and the dinosaur family celebrated Hanukkah, a segment Reubens continues to be proud of.

"I believe that was one of the first times you had Hanukkah represented on a television Christmas special," Reubens said in the show's DVD commentary track.

Fenton was particularly tickled when she was assigned to show the food in the refrigerator celebrating and drinking eggnog by sticking a straw into an egg.

"It was really fun to decorate the refrigerator for Christmas," Fenton explains. "Of course you would have a grape tree."

Art directors Ric Heitzman, Wayne White, and Jimmy Cuomo created a new outdoor set for the special, complete with an ice-skating rink and pounds of plastic snow. Although the creative team initially planned on building a real ice-skating rink on the set, director Wayne Orr came up with an easier solution that was also easy on the budget.

"I worked on *The Donny and Marie Show* where they had an ice rink, so I knew what

© Craig Shimala

© Sarah Llewllyn

Playhouse fans opening gifts on Christmas morning

that entailed," Orr recalls. "It was a very big deal. I was concerned about that and [about] our financial situation. There was no place to get an ice rink that was financially reasonable. I had heard of a plastic that could be laid down on the floor that people can actually skate on, so we went out on a search and I found a place out into the Valley that did have this. It was a lifesaver. It was just large sheets of plastic that are linked together and you can actually skate quite nicely on it. It was a great save to find something like that because you are not concerned about what the temperature in the building is and it's just a ridiculous difference in cost."

Pee-wee's Playhouse Christmas Special has the unique distinction of being the only episode in which the characters venture into Puppetland. As a result, the eight-foot-tall playhouse model from the opening credits makes a special appearance in exterior shots. The model can be seen best during the sequence when Pee-wee makes tracks in the snow and attempts to hide from Cowboy Curtis.

The show's creative team was well aware they were creating a visual feast for the viewing audience.

"We figure the hardcore *Playhouse* fans will flip out," Binder said in an interview leading up to the show's broadcast. "Just decorating the playhouse lends itself to the whole fantasy aspect of a Christmas special."

The opening musical number, "Oh, It's Christmas in the Playhouse," is one of the show's most memorable moments, but surprisingly, the sequence almost didn't happen. Reubens and Paragon wrote into the script that a choir of children would open the show dressed as angels. During the first preproduction meeting for the special, Orr expressed his displeasure with the idea.

"I said, 'Geez, I don't know, but that sounds a little kind of precious to me,'" Orr recalls. "'It doesn't really sound like the *Playhouse*. How about if we had some sort of military glee club from the army or the Marines or something? A group of guys in uniform in the playhouse sounds immediately funny to me.' They totally got behind that right away."

Binder put out a search for a military glee club, but they were all booked. He decided to go in a different direction, offering the UCLA Men's Choir the opportunity to be in the special dressed as Marines. However, there was a catch.

"They had to shave off their facial hair," Binder says. "I was shocked when they said they would do it to be in the show!"

After the show aired, Binder received a very special long-distance telephone call in his Los Angeles office.

"I got a telephone call after the show aired from the commander of the Marine Corps out of Washington, D.C.," Binder recalls. "He called me to officially reprimand us for impersonating Marines and to tell me how embarrassing it was to them. He went through this whole speech, and after he said, 'Okay, that's the official thing. The unofficial thing is that my kids loved it.'"

The UCLA choir learned their choreography for the opening number in a few hours and the sequence was shot later that morning. Niki Haris, Madonna's longtime backup singer, appeared in the opening musical number as one of Pee-wee's backup singers, sporting a Supremes-style wig and gold sequin dress.

Although the sequence isn't the version that he and Paragon had originally planned, it is Reubens' favorite part of the special.

"From the animated beginning through naming all the live-action characters, all the guest stars, all the puppets with that music and that choir," Reubens said excitedly on the Christmas special DVD commentary. "It doesn't get any better than that."

PEE-WEE'S CHRISTMAS GUESTS

Pee-wee's Playhouse Christmas Special is best remembered for its guest stars — a combination of retro icons and mega-celebrities of the day. Frankie Avalon, Charo, Cher, the Del Rubio Triplets, Annette Funicello, Zsa Zsa Gabor, Whoopi Goldberg, Magic Johnson, Grace Jones, k.d. lang, Little Richard, Joan Rivers, Dinah Shore, and Oprah Winfrey all made appearances.

"We just made up a wish list of people [we wanted], and then we got every single person on that list," Reubens says. "So it was really great, especially on not a lot of notice. A few people changed their plans to be able to be on it."

Having special guest stars allowed the show's creative team to finally appease some of the celebrities who had long wanted to be on the show, some since its first season — it also broadened the appeal of the show to include a more adult audience.

"You put Grace Jones on any show and you're opening yourself up to cutting-edge television," Binder says.

Pee-wee on Joan Rivers' short-lived late-night show

"To say we had an eclectic group of guest stars is kind of an understatement," Reubens said at the time.

While Pee-wee's guest stars were all enthusiastic about being on the special, not all of the celebrities were able to make the trip to the playhouse. Because of scheduling constraints, Oprah Winfrey's cameo was shot in Chicago, and Joan Rivers' was filmed on the set of *The Hollywood Squares*.

Zsa Zsa Gabor, who appears in a brief scene with the Cowntess, got under the skin of George McGrath, the actor who provided the puppet's voice.

"Zsa Zsa was crazy," he recalls. "She loved to improvise, which would have been great except nothing she ad-libbed made any sense. She was by far the biggest pain in the ass of [all] the celebrities."

Magic Johnson's cameo appearance as Magic Screen's distant cousin had to be shot in less than an hour because he had a basketball game against the Lakers later that evening.

As rushed as Johnson's appearance was, it was an eternity when compared to Cher's brief time on the set. Orr was able to leverage a connection with her management in order to get the singer to make an appearance at the playhouse. The shoot was shoehorned in between appearances to promote her Uninhibited perfume.

"We basically set everything up for Cher," recalls John Paragon. "Cher was in there for twenty-five minutes and then she was gone."

Even though her time was limited, she left a lasting impression on the cast and crew. Puppeteer Kevin Carlson, who shared a scene with her as Conky, calls his time filming with

George McGrath and Cher on the Christmas special set

Cher "the coolest moment of my time working on the show."

George McGrath, who voiced a number of the puppets during the special, also says meeting Cher was his favorite thing that ever happened at the *Playhouse*.

"I brought my Cher doll," he recalls. "She signed it. I said, 'You know, I'm a big fan of yours,' and she said, 'Yes, I guess so. Not many people bring the doll around.'"

Little Richard accidentally pulled Magic Screen's arm off during one of his takes. Even though the artist only made a brief appearance in the special, he was conscientious about his performance.

"He said, 'You want me to scream like a white woman or a black woman?'" Paragon recalls, in reference to the shriek the performer lets out when he falls during ice-skating.

Grace Jones, Dinah Shore, the Del Rubio Triplets, k.d. lang, and Charo all performed new arrangements of classic Christmas songs on the special.

"We tried to do nontraditional things with traditional songs, while still keeping the show in the spirit of the holiday," Reubens later told *Newsday*. "I didn't want people to think I was satirizing a Christmas special."

Grace Jones, never one to shy away from an opportunity to make a unique fashion statement, wore an outfit created by an avant-garde Japanese designer.

"That hat was just a piece of foam with a slit in it," Reubens joked on the DVD's commentary track. "We should have taught kids how to make it. That would have been a good thing to do."

Her rendition of "The Little Drummer Boy" was an arrangement she had received from David Bowie. The two were sitting next to each other on a plane shortly after Jones agreed to be on the special. She asked Bowie what she should sing and he suggested the song. A few weeks later he mailed her a track with an arrangement she could use just for the special.

Although her performance went off without a hitch, Jones's reputation as a diva was a concern to some of the show's creative team.

"The word was just 'Why would you get Grace Jones? She is really difficult to work with,'" Orr recalls. "Everybody who was a guest, including Grace Jones, just absolutely left any baggage outside the studio. They could not have been nicer."

However, off the set, Jones caused a financial problem. "I was shocked at the charges Grace Jones billed us at her hotel when she checked out," Binder recalls.

Even though Dinah Shore's extended rendition of "The Twelve Days of Christmas" was sung over the picture phone, the sequence was actually shot in the playhouse kitchen.

"Someone was in the kitchen with Dinah," Reubens joked at the time.

Shore was initially hesitant about appearing on the show, but agreed after producers complied with her one request.

"I didn't want to sit on Chairry," Shore recalls.

But her concerns were quickly put aside. The singer later told puppeteer Alison Mork that the talking chair was her favorite character.

"She was so willing to make fun and be such a good sport," Reubens recalled on the DVD commentary track. "She so got the joke."

Shore's segment was shot on videotape while the rest of the special was shot on film. Although Shore nailed her performance, Orr was unhappy with the way the video and film were integrated.

"I was really disappointed with the video phone segments," Orr recalls. "Dinah's people told me to take particular care of how she looked. She looked great on the set, but I was very disappointed at the way it was filmed."

Although Orr noticed the difference between the way Shore looked on set and on television, he never heard from her management or from Dinah herself.

"I don't know if they ever saw it," he says. "I don't know if it was high on her must-see list."

The Del Rubio Triplets, a musical act of three middle-aged sisters in miniskirts who performed acoustic versions of pop songs, performed a quirky rendition of "Winter Wonderland." The trio had gained a cult following after a number of sitcom appearances on shows like *Full House*, *Married…With Children*, and *The Golden Girls*. Reubens was so impressed with the group that they were invited to appear in the first episode of the fourth season. Although Reubens loved their act, not everyone involved with the special was in on the joke. "The Del Rubio Triplets were an act I never got," McGrath says. "But Paul seemed to love them."

Before agreeing to appear on the special, k.d. lang made a request to Binder. "She wanted to do something different," Binder recalls. "She didn't want to just stand and sing by herself."

Ultimately, she performed "Jingle Bell Rock" with Dirty Dog, Cool Cat, and Chicky Baby serving as her band. Her sequence took nearly half a day to film, the longest in the show.

Courtesy PhotoFest

Charo

Reubens had met Charo in Hawaii while writing *Big Top Pee-wee*. He briefly flirted with the idea of writing a *Pee-wee's Playhouse Goes Hawaiian* special, which would have involved the singer, but he scrapped the idea. Instead, when it came time to contact celebrities about the Christmas special, Reubens called Charo personally to ask for her participation.

Charo, who sang live during multiple takes, also made a striking impression on the cast and crew.

"The amazing thing about Charo is, when you meet her, she's exactly like she is on television," Paragon recalls. "She's really charming."

Of all the special guest stars, Frankie Avalon and Annette Funicello spent the most time on the playhouse set. The two met Reubens on the set of their 1987 film *Back to the Beach*. Pee-wee appeared briefly in the film to perform The Trashmen's 1963 hit song "Surfin' Bird."

Reubens had been a lifelong fan of the duo, so he really enjoyed another opportunity to work with his childhood heroes.

"When [Paul] appeared in our movie, he told me that his dream was to be a Mouseketeer," Funicello recalls.

"Paul was just so excited to have them on," Orr recalls. "He was really, really happy that they could do it for us, and they just absolutely got into it."

Frankie and Annette got along famously together. Alison Mork noticed their strong connection while filming the last sequence, when Santa Claus comes to the playhouse.

"When we would cut between takes, Frankie wouldn't let go of Annette's hand," Mork recalls fondly. "It was really clear that they were really good friends."

Whoopi Goldberg was the last celebrity to be booked on the special. Although she wasn't on the writers' initial wish list, Reubens heard she was taping an episode of the short-lived program *D.C. Follies* on a neighboring soundstage and he personally invited her to be in the

Courtesy Paramount Pictures / PhotoFest © Paramount Pictures

Pee-wee joins Frankie and Annette in *Back to the Beach*

special. A big fan of William Marshall's performance in *Blacula*, Goldberg was disappointed to find out that the King of Cartoons was not on the set her day of filming.

The decision to contract more than a dozen guest stars to perform in a single special might have resulted in disaster for the cast and crew, but the filming went off without a hitch.

"They all worked hard," Orr recalls of the guest stars. "They loved being there. They would go around and look at the various puppets and things like that and they just totally got into the magic of the playhouse. It shows that everybody was having a good time. They became kids again, I guess.

COAL IN PEE-WEE'S STOCKING

The producers and CBS planned an aggressive promotional campaign for the special, with Reubens and several of the guest stars giving telephone interviews from the set to journalists around the country. Reubens talked about the special, but he also continued damage control, explaining away his poor box office returns for *Big Top Pee-wee*.

"I like the movie a lot," Reubens said during a 1988 interview. "I think it's got a lot of funny stuff in it. I think maybe people just weren't prepared for me to take such a big leap, ya know, as far as me becoming a leading man."

Some critics wondered whether *Pee-wee's Playhouse Christmas Special* would join the long-standing tradition of televised holiday specials or if it would fail to connect with the general public. With the stakes raised, Reubens needed his special to do big business.

More than nine million people watched the show on Wednesday, December 21, 1988, at 8 p.m., a mediocre viewing audience for the time slot (only 17 percent of all televisions turned on during that hour were tuned in to the special). The airing didn't even crack the top 50 for the week and was a disappointment for CBS, whose execs had been hoping the special would give them a much-needed boost with a younger demographic in prime time.

"I think they were a little disappointed it didn't get the adult ratings they were hoping for," Binder recalls. "There wasn't any criticism of the creative content; it was just questioning whether Paul had primetime chops."

According to Judy Price, then the vice president in charge of children's programming at CBS, the special may have suffered because it deviated too far from the formula that made the show successful on Saturday mornings.

"The Christmas special wasn't one of my favorites," she says. "It wasn't really a big commercial success. It didn't get big ratings. I think it sort of got carried away by its star power. It was gratuitous."

While *Pee-wee's Playhouse Christmas Special* might have been a disappointment to the network executives, it remains a standout in the series among *Playhouse* fans. The special has been released in three home video formats in 1988, 1996, and 2004 (laserdisc, VHS, and DVD, respectively) and has aired on Fox Family, MTV, and Cartoon Network. In recent years, Pee-wee Herman's official website has allowed fans to stream the special for free during the holiday season.

Despite the ratings of the initial airing of the special, the cast and crew remain proud of their work on the show.

"The Christmas show itself, I thought, was very clever," Binder says. "It still holds up."

5 | FORECLOSURE

© Ken Sax

ALTHOUGH THE CHRISTMAS special rejuvenated the *Playhouse* cast and crew, Reubens was exhausted from the rigors of so many Pee-wee Herman projects. He was ready to let go of his Saturday morning timeslot. It had been fairly easy for Judy Price to get Reubens to renew his contract for two years in 1987, but she knew she would have to work harder to secure the show for a fourth and fifth season.

© Ken Sax

"I told him he would have to do two more seasons if he was thinking of having a package he could sell into syndication," she explains. "That was always the goal of anyone doing a series. You have to build enough of a library in order to syndicate so you continue to make money from the show. But it was a huge commitment for him because he was involved in every aspect."

In order to reach the minimum number of episodes required for a syndication package, Reubens would have had to produce 14 additional *Playhouse* episodes, which would have been more than the 10 to 13 episodes required for one season of a children's show. Price proposed that Reubens film 20 episodes in one year, deliver them all to CBS, and they would air half of those episodes for the 1989–1990 season and air the rest the following year. That would not only give Reubens enough episodes for syndication, but it would give him a much-needed break from Pee-wee Herman. After considering the offer, Reubens accepted.

Before Reubens continued on the show's fourth and fifth seasons, he changed producers for the second time in three years. Steve Binder, who had produced the second and third seasons of the series as well as the Christmas special, was let go from the show without warning. He was replaced by the production team of Sonny Grosso and Larry Jacobson.

"Paul never confronted me," Binder says. "He had his lawyer phone me and tell me that his manager had decided to bring in another production company."

Instead of contracting staff writers to work on the entire season, Reubens and the producers hired a number of freelance writers to come up with individual scripts. This freed Reubens and John Paragon, who was a regular writer, to codirect

© Ken Sax

the last two seasons. However, even with what may have been perceived as fewer on-set responsibilities, Reubens was still exhausted. As a result, the *Playhouse* writers were encouraged to come up with plots that centered on secondary characters, to add longer classic cartoons, and to show more educational videos, all in an attempt to limit Pee-wee's time on screen. These

strategies were regularly employed during the show's fourth and fifth seasons, but in fact, Reubens had occasionally asked the writers to limit his screen time in earlier seasons, if his workload became too heavy.

"There was one episode we had written in which Paul was going to do a Patty Duke sort of thing, playing Pee-wee and his country cousin," George McGrath remembers. "During production, at the last minute, Paul decided he didn't want to do it because it was going to be too exhausting. I had to write a new episode over the weekend."

One of the first public signs of Reubens' fatigue arose in early 1989, when the actor gave an interview to Jane Wollman of *Newsday* on the show's set. He was dressed in costume, and his sit-down was conducted during breaks in the shooting schedule. But, for the first time in over five years, the actor spoke without the character's assistance.

"When you work twelve hours a day, you have no personal life," Reubens said — as himself. "I'm up at five in the morning and on the set by seven. By the time I get home at eight, take a shower, and eat dinner, it's already past my bedtime. It's built into my schedule that I can't get enough sleep."

Despite his fatigue with the show, Reubens and his creative team came up with new ways to entertain their audience. The playhouse welcomed a new puppet character, a talking chandelier with a French accent (provided by Alison Mork), and a new animated segment called El Hombre, which featured a Latino superhero who fights crime in the inner city. The cartoon, which was illustrated on a black velvet canvas, was inspired by a painting Reubens had hung in his office.

Bill Freiberger, who wrote the segments, says, "I remember Prudence and I went to Olvera Street to find a copy of the painting to base it on. Ultimately, we ended up drawing our own version of it."

While the sequences were stylistically different from anything else on the show, El Hombre had the unique distinction of being broadcast completely in Spanish without any English translations. According to Freiberger, this decision was an excellent example of the show's central thesis.

"The basic message of the show was: accept everyone, no matter who they are," he says. "That comes through in all the crazy characters that were in the show. I think El Hombre was Paul's way of opening it up even more and making it more inclusive to people of different ethnic backgrounds."

The 20-episode shoot went smoothly and, although Judy Price was doubtful that Reubens would sign on for two more seasons, she once again offered him the opportunity to renew through to 1993. Although he appreciated the offer, Paul Reubens felt he was finally beginning to burn out. The playhouse would go into foreclosure after the fifth season.

"Directing, producing, writing, and acting all at once is really exhausting," Reubens said in a 1989 interview.

"He'd just felt like he'd done it," said Michael McLean, Reubens' agent at the time.

"Paul was exhausted," Lynne Stewart recalls. "He was doing everything and that starts to wear on someone."

Even the most casual onlooker would acknowledge that what Reubens had done was nothing short of astonishing. In five years, he had reached a level of fame that most comedians only dream of. He had successfully transitioned his career from an underground cult icon to the king of Saturday morning television. *Pee-wee's Playhouse* had definitely defied the odds, inviting nearly 10 million viewers every Saturday morning into a wonderland of talking furniture, stop-motion animation, and kaleidoscopic sets. The show had been nominated for 38 Emmy Awards in five short years and it had totally redefined what a Saturday morning program could be, let alone what an audience for a Saturday morning show could look like.

On November 10, 1990, almost a year after the final episode was actually filmed, fans at home watched as Pee-wee Herman walked up his art deco, ice blue floor, pulled the arm of the Greek statue resting on a small white shelf, and walked over to his cherry red scooter that was emerging from behind a trick wall. He picked up his helmet, adorned with purple wings and a giant Cyclops eye, stepped on the scooter, and gazed directly at the viewing audience.

"The playhouse will always be here for everyone to play in forever and ever and ever," Pee-wee said. "On that you have my WORD."

Pee-wee had said the secret word, just as he had at the end of every episode. Beyond the playhouse, in living rooms, college dormitories, and restaurants across the nation, nearly 10 million people yelled back at their television sets in response for the final time.

©Ken Sax

With that, Pee-wee focused his eyes off-camera. The scooter ejected from its place, toward an adjacent wall, which opened as he raced toward it, projecting him out of the playhouse, over Mount Rushmore, off to a destination unknown.

After filming wrapped for the fifth and final season, the cast and crew went their separate ways. Most of the animators went on to different projects, citing *Pee-wee's Playhouse* as a door-opener to future opportunities. John Singleton, a production assistant on the show, went on to direct Larry Fishburne in 1991's *Boyz n the Hood*. The film made Singleton, 24 years old at the time of the film's release, the youngest person ever to be nominated in the Best Director category at the Academy Awards. Fishburne (after changing his name from Larry to Laurence) went on to critical acclaim with lead roles in *What's Love Got to Do with It* and *The Matrix*. S. Epatha Merkerson went on to star in *Law & Order* for 17 seasons, appearing in 390 episodes in total. The remainder of the show's cast and crew took on other projects, spent time with family, and caught up on some much-needed rest.

Like Pee-wee, Reubens' post-*Playhouse* destination was also unknown. He began his hiatus traveling to Italy, Hawaii, and Florida with friends.

"All we did was just get in the van and drive," says songwriter Allee Willis, a friend of

Reubens. "[That] year was about taking off and figuring out what the next move was. He had some great ideas, but not a concrete plan."

"It was time to take a year off," Reubens recalls. "I had actually made a list of things I wanted to do — learn Spanish, learn to play the sax — and I never hit one of them. At the end of [1990, while season five was airing], I decided I was going to take a second year off. That didn't exactly go the way I planned."

"THE INCIDENT"

By now, what derailed Reubens' career has become a part of pop culture infamy. In the evening of Friday, July 26, 1991, while visiting his parents in Sarasota, Reubens was arrested in the lobby of an adult movie theater for indecent exposure. Overnight, Pee-wee Herman went from the country's most popular jokester to its biggest joke.

The media's reaction to the arrest was brutal. The *New York Post* ran a front-page story with the headline, "Oh, Pee-wee!" with a small picture of Reubens in character and a large photo of his mug shot from the Sarasota police department. The difference between the two images was startling. Pee-wee's crew cut was replaced by Reubens' stringy black hair that flowed past his shoulders. His once-shaven face now had a full goatee. His trademark gray suit had been

replaced by a white T-shirt, and his colorful playhouse backdrop had been exchanged for cold, gray cinderblock.

Throughout the show's run, Reubens had gone to great pains to hide his true identity from the public, believing that the character worked better if the public thought Pee-wee was a real person. While Reubens' name can be found throughout the credits of his various projects in technical roles, Pee-wee Herman was always listed as "himself."

But as news of what many on the show still refer to simply as "the incident" circulated around the nation, the public's reaction to Reubens' arrest snowballed beyond control and expectation. Late-night comedians peppered their monologues with cringe-worthy jokes, and parents made hundreds of telephone calls to *Playhouse* advertisers expressing their displeasure over what had happened.

In turn, these advertisers pressured the CBS network to withdraw the last five reruns of *Playhouse* that were to be broadcast before the fall season began.

"One thing about children's television, particularly at that time before the proliferation of cable and edgier fare for children, was that any hint of scandal could be ruinous," Judy Price explains. "Most of the advertising was purchased before the seasons aired and the sponsors were guaranteed a certain season average rating. The fact that *Pee-wee's Playhouse* [had completed its run and] was in reruns was irrelevant. If we didn't make good on our end in regards to ratings, we would have had to reimburse the advertisers and it would have meant a financial loss for the network."

© Ken Sax

Although it had been announced that the series wasn't going to return for a sixth season, Pee-wee's premature departure from the airwaves led many to wrongly believe that the network had canceled the show in the wake of the controversy.

"I was pissed off at how many times I saw it reported that CBS had canceled the series," George McGrath remembers. "Paul had already ended the series. It was just sloppy reporting that made it look like Paul lost a lot more career-wise than he actually did. That false impression that the *Playhouse* would have gone on longer if it hadn't been for his arrest is still the common perception of what happened. It still pisses me off a little."

"It is frustrating that the same myth gets published over and over," Reubens said in an interview with *Entertainment Weekly*. "CBS didn't cancel the show. I'd already been away from the show a year and a half. You go from Pee-wee's picture to that mug shot . . . I get that it was a good story. A lot of people wrote, 'He's ruined his career. Pee-wee's dead.' I never said anything like that."

There has long been speculation about what led CBS to pull the remaining *Playhouse* episodes. While a great deal of misinformation has been disseminated in the media, Judy Price is glad to set the record straight on what actually occurred in the days after the story broke.

"CBS's reaction initially was not severe," she continues. "I saw the story on the eleven o'clock news on Saturday night, and Paul wasn't recognizable. He had a beard, goatee, and long hair. I knew, because I had been in children's television long enough, that there was going to be a problem."

Price attempted to do damage control before the media had a field day with the story.

"The next morning I called the head of our press department and told her about what happened," she continues. "She just sort of dismissed it and didn't think it would be a big deal. Then on Monday, I spoke with Jeff Sagansky, the chief of CBS Entertainment at the time, who wasn't alarmed because Paul hadn't been proven guilty of anything."

The blanket of ambivalence around the network started to lift as time passed.

"Throughout the day, calls started coming in from our affiliates and advertisers," she remembers. "Of course, the press was all over us. It was obvious the backlash had started. Everyone was trying to get statements. I started preparing to put something else on the air that weekend because I knew eventually I would be ordered to, even though everyone kept saying it wasn't

© John Duke Kisch / CBS

a problem. But then I got a call from Howard Stringer, president of the network. He didn't tell me directly what to do, but he indicated we had a problem. The affiliates were threatening to dump the show and the advertisers were ready to jump ship. In order to take the heat off them, we decided to pull the show so we would be the bad guys instead."

Price remembers making the phone call to Reubens' team to inform them of the news.

"I did have a conversation with Paul's people, but there was no debate or discussion," she explains. "It was going off the air. It wasn't that we canceled the show, it was just that we didn't carry it for the last four or five weeks of its run."

Although she knew the story would garner media attention, Price was frustrated by the legs the story had.

"This news about the show ended up taking great pressure off George H.W. Bush, who was president at the time, because we were having major issues with unemployment, but *Pee-wee's Playhouse* was dominating the headlines," she says. "I was dismayed that this became such a story, but I wasn't surprised. The public eats up titillating stories. I'm guilty of it, too. Something will catch your eye and you tend to read it. That's what people do. They like to see scandal and the ugly side of their stars. And it was a feeding-frenzy, believe me. I didn't take or do interviews at the time because what was I going to say?"

While she doesn't totally believe news outlets like *Rolling Stone* that hypothesized that Reubens deliberately went into the theater to sabotage his career, Price does believe "the incident" might have been motivated by an unconscious desire to take a break.

"I felt bad for Paul, but on the other hand, some people thought it was him deliberately trying to kill the character. I don't even think the arresting officer would have recognized him had Paul not identified himself as being Pee-wee Herman. I don't believe that's why he went out there, but perhaps subconsciously [it was], because he wasn't set on working all that hard at that time. He had achieved great success and accolades with *Pee-wee's Playhouse* and that certainly made him feel good. He accomplished something with it, but at the same time, he was ready to move on."

As CBS pulled the remaining episodes, other efforts were being made to expunge Pee-wee from the national record. Toy stores were yanking merchandise off the shelves, inadvertently making the Pee-wee Herman doll an instant collector's item. Therapists and social workers were taking to the television airwaves and newspapers to counsel parents on how to break the news of Reubens' arrest to children. By today's standards, the story might have captivated the public's interest for a few days, but in 1991, it was an around-the-clock public crucifixion.

However, as most people jumped on the anti-Pee-wee bandwagon, protests were being held in New York, Los Angeles, and San Francisco arguing against CBS's pulling of the show.

Courtesy PhotoFest

Many celebrities, including Bill Cosby, Cyndi Lauper, and Joan Rivers, also went on record in support of their colleague.

"He has given so much pleasure to little kids, and what they're doing to him is sad," said Annette Funicello at the time. "I like him a lot. If I were able to call him now, I would say, 'So many people are on your side. We love you. Just hang in there — it will blow over. These things do.'"

During all this, Reubens lay low, humiliated by what had transpired.

"Paul, who is emotionally devastated by the embarrassment of this situation, is currently in seclusion with friends and eagerly anticipating his complete vindication," his publicist Richard Grant said at the time.

The "complete vindication" Reubens hoped for never came because the actor accepted a plea bargain. Once he had entered a plea of no contest, the actor was ordered to perform 75 hours community service, to write, produce, and cover the production costs of an anti-drug public service announcement, and pay a $50 fine and court costs.

Although Reubens had hoped that avoiding a trial would put an end to the media scrutiny, it turns out he had misjudged the public. Except for a few special appearances, when Reubens left the courtroom on November 7, 1991, he left Pee-wee Herman behind him.

6 | P2K

ON THE EVENING of July 10, 1999, Paul Reubens made his first talk show appearance ever as himself. His visit to *The Tonight Show with Jay Leno* was a resounding success, and the actor received a hero's welcome when he walked out on stage. Tremors of laughter rippled through the audience whenever glimpses of Pee-wee radiated through Reubens' words and mannerisms. Although the actor was promoting his upcoming appearance in *Mystery Men*, three sentences spoken softly at the end of his appearance sent shockwaves across the newswires and Internet.

"I start next week writing a new movie called *The Pee-wee Herman Story*," he said. "It's a movie about fame. Pee-wee Herman becomes famous in this movie and turns into a monster."

News that Pee-wee Herman was coming out of retirement was astonishing. Since "the incident," Reubens had kept a relatively low profile, taking roles in *Batman Returns* and the original *Buffy the Vampire Slayer* movie. He earned an Emmy Award nomination in 1995 for his guest appearances on *Murphy Brown*. Though Reubens continued to stand at the edges of the spotlight, Pee-wee was nowhere to be seen. Barring a 1991 cameo at the MTV Video Music Awards, where he famously alluded to his arrest by asking if the audience had "heard any good jokes lately," and an appearance a year later at a Grand Old Opry tribute to Minnie Pearl, the "luckiest boy in the world" had become the most reclusive.

However, Reubens' Leno appearance seemed to signal that his leave of absence was ending. Throughout the following decade, the actor made dozens of public appearances, talking up his upcoming Pee-wee films — a second one based on *Pee-wee's Playhouse* was announced in 2004 — along the way, whetting the appetites of his fans worldwide who had expected they'd never see Pee-wee again.

In interviews Reubens described *The Pee-wee Herman Story* as dark and closer in tone to *Valley of the Dolls* than the brightness and whimsy of *Pee-wee's Big Adventure* and *Big Top Pee-wee*.

Courtesy CBS / PhotoFest © CBS

Paul Reubens with Candice Bergen on *Murphy Brown*

The film's plot centers on Pee-wee making it big as a country singer and stepping on his friends on the way to the top of the charts. Along the way, Pee-wee acquires habits that clash with the squeaky-clean image he projected on Saturday morning.

"Pee-wee Herman winds up getting hooked on pills and booze," Reubens explained in 2001. "[Pee-wee's] not shooting up, but I wouldn't want young kids to see it."

Reubens cowrote the film with Valerie Curtin, the screenwriter behind *…And Justice for All* starring Al Pacino and *Toys* starring Robin Williams. He cited the film's plot as being a hybrid of elements from *It Could Happen to You*, *Jailhouse Rock*, and *A Face in the Crowd*.

While Reubens has maintained that the film is only a "fake autobiography," Dawna Kaufmann, who first brought the playhouse concept to the then-standup comic in 1980, sees similarities between the fiction and reality. In *A Face in the Crowd*, a convict named Lonesome Rhodes is discovered by a female producer who makes him a star. By the film's climax, Rhodes, played brilliantly by Andy Griffith in his cinematic debut, becomes a national superstar, affecting popular culture like no celebrity before him. Ultimately, the producer deflates the hot air from his balloon by turning a microphone on during one of Rhodes' rants about how he thinks his fans are all idiotic sheep, exposing him for the heartless beast he's become.

According to Kaufmann, Reubens was infatuated with the film during the time the two worked together.

"When we would have writing sessions at his home for *The Pee-wee Herman Show*, we would take a break by watching the movie," she says. "Paul would always stop the tape and rewind it just before the producer exposed him for the villain he truly was. He didn't want to see that part. He just wanted to see Lonesome Rhodes going from nowhere, becoming a big star, and stepping on everyone around him. I should have taken the hint."

As more details became available about the adult Pee-wee film, Reubens announced he was revisiting his playhouse for a second, more kid-friendly film. *Pee-wee's Playhouse: The Movie* was allegedly greenlit by Paramount Pictures, although those statements seem to have been exaggerations at best. The film would have teamed the actor up with a new host of crazy characters, along with some familiar friends.

In adapting the children's show for the big screen, Reubens' script took the characters outside of the playhouse walls and into the real world.

"In the TV show, we never left the playhouse," Reubens explained in 2010. "You never saw Puppetland. I mean, me and Cowboy Curtis went camping one time. There's a couple episodes where you went, 'Where are they?' but most of the time we were in the playhouse. The movie has two scenes in the playhouse, at the beginning and the end, and the rest of the movie takes place outside."

The movie begins on a normal day, with Conky giving the secret word and the King of Cartoons coming over to screen a classic animated short. However, that's a short-lived moment of comfort before the real adventure begins.

"In the opening of the movie, right in the middle of the cartoon, the film jams, it burns, it's blacked out," Reubens elaborated in the same interview. "When the lights come back up, the King is gone. He's been kidnapped and is being held hostage for ransom by a character named El Chunky Boobabi."

The film's structure closely resembles an original draft of a film called *Pee-wee's Big Adventure* that was pitched to, and ultimately rejected by, Paramount Studios, which Reubens cowrote with Gary Panter in 1983, two years after the close of *The Pee-wee Herman Show*. Although the title was later used for the character's bicycle film, the Reubens-Panter script had many of the characters from the live show embarking on a road trip through Puppetland. Optimistic that he would have an opportunity to bring that film to the screen after the success of *Playhouse*, Reubens had rewritten the script several times since 1990, incorporating characters like Chairry, Conky, and Magic Screen who weren't a part of the live show. He renamed the film *Pee-wee's Playhouse: The Movie*.

Reubens has admitted that he'd consider casting another actor as Pee-wee Herman. Although he has joked in recent years that *Twilight's* Taylor Lautner was in negotiations to fill his tasseled white loafers, Reubens seriously offered Johnny Depp the opportunity to be his successor.

"Could you imagine Johnny as Pee-wee?" asks Prudence Fenton, *Playhouse* animation and effects producer. "That'd be hilarious."

PEE-WEE COMES OUT OF RETIREMENT

Although he had been mentioning that Pee-wee Herman was due to make a comeback, Reubens shocked his fans when he announced in early August 2009 that he would be returning to the stage for a revival of *The Pee-wee Herman Show*. The show was scheduled to run from November 19 to 29 in a limited engagement at the Music Box at The Fonda in Hollywood.

At the Twitter Conference in 2009 where Pee-wee had his first public appearance since announcing his comeback

"I've put part of him away for a long time, but part of him has always been here with me," Reubens told the *Los Angeles Times*. "I think it will be like riding a bike — which isn't a bad analogy for Pee-wee, by the way."

Although Pee-wee Herman had gone into seclusion, Reubens had kept up the hope that the character would have an opportunity to reappear.

"I spent an awful long time twelve years ago thinking to myself, you know, this can't

© Brian Solis

be my final thing," Reubens said in a 2004 *Dateline* interview. "I'm a big believer in the happy ending. I want a Pee-wee movie to have a happy ending, Pee-wee gets his bicycle back. I don't know what the ending is to my story, but I think it's going to be a happy one."

For a while it appeared doubtful that Reubens' career would have the happy ending he sought. After returning to the spotlight in the late 1990s, the actor attracted attention for a featured role as a gay, drug-dealing hairdresser in the 2001 film *Blow*. Although the role was a departure from the more comedic roles audiences were used to, his performance won the respect of critics. *Esquire* summed the film up best: "There are many reasons to see *Blow* . . . but perhaps the best reason is to see Paul Reubens, who hasn't had a role worthy of his talents since the glorious, pre-scandal days of Pee-wee Herman."

Reubens seemed poised for a full-scale comeback until a 2002 arrest that was nearly fatal to his career. Acting on an anonymous tip, the Los Angeles police department searched

Reubens' home for child pornography. The actor pled guilty to a single misdemeanor count for possession of obscene material. Many of his fans believe the arrest was spurious and, unlike the passive way he responded publicly to "the incident," Reubens hit the airwaves to clear his name with his supporters.

"One thing I want to make very, very clear," he said in an interview after his arrest. "I don't want anyone for one second to think that I am titillated by images of children. It's not me. You can say lots of things about me, and you might. The public may think I'm weird. They may think I'm crazy or anything that anyone wants to think about me. That's all fine, as long as one of the things you're not thinking about me is that I'm a pedophile, because that's not true."

The public's response seemed to suggest that Reubens would have the chance to accomplish everything else he wanted to with the character. He hoped to see another Pee-wee Herman film in theaters and introduce the character to a new generation. If things went well with the live show at The Music Box, he thought, maybe someone in Hollywood would give him another shot.

While attempting to drum up interest in his films, the actor had floated another trial balloon to test how the public would react to a Pee-wee return. In 2007, Reubens put on his classic costume for the first time in 15 years to appear at the Spike TV Guys' Choice Awards. Although Reubens was out of practice with the character, the packed audience at the event applauded wildly when he stepped out on stage and the appearance was considered a success by those in the media.

The idea to bring Pee-wee back to the stage was not Reubens', but Broadway producer Jared Geller's. Geller was a longtime fan who thought a live show could spark a resurgence in the character's career. Initially the actor refused, but just as the barrage of phone calls had worked in the summer of 1986 to get Reubens rolling on his CBS Saturday morning show, Reubens ultimately changed his mind.

"I went back and forth between wanting to do it and not wanting to do it," Reubens said in a 2009 interview with the *L.A. Times*. "I had a producer that was calling me every two months for two years and every two months, I would change my mind. Finally, one day I woke up and decided, 'This is it, I'm coming back.'"

In order to build publicity for his upcoming performances, ID Public Relations, the firm founded by Reubens' new manager Kelly Bush, created a public Facebook page and Twitter account for Pee-wee's fans to reconnect with the character. Almost overnight, Pee-wee Herman was an Internet sensation. This gave him the ability to connect with his fans directly for the first time in his 30-year career.

© Brian Solis

Pee-wee with Kelly Bush and Natalie Lent of ID Public Relations

The original idea for the revival of *The Pee-wee Herman Show* was to use the script from the show that ran at the Groundling Theatre and The Roxy in 1981 and to make minor edits so the show was more relevant to a contemporary audience. Out of respect for the late Phil Hartman, who had been tragically murdered by his wife in 1998, Kap'n Karl was replaced by Cowboy Curtis, a character created after the stage production had finished. A number of original cast members, like Lynne Stewart, John Paragon, and John Moody, who was Mailman Mike, were also invited to return.

On August 17, 2009, the first staged reading for potential investors took place at Alley Kat Studios in Hollywood. Reubens requested the help of *Playhouse* alum Ric Heitzman, George McGrath, and Alison Mork. To avoid unwanted attention, the show was listed as *Mr. Bungle: The Musical*, a reference to the 1959 educational film that had been shown during the original live show.

"At the first table reading the script was almost exactly the same show," McGrath recalls. "Joan Leizman was going to be reprising her role as the hypnotized audience member and the musical salute to Sly Stone was still there. The biggest difference was that an actor dressed as Susan Boyle [from *Britain's Got Talent*] was going to start the show with 'The Star-Spangled Banner.'"

As Reubens continued to work on the script, he and the show's producers were caught by surprise when The Music Box reported they had sold nearly 10,000 tickets to the show in 24 hours. People from around the world were buying tickets and planning to fly in to Los Angeles for the 10-day run. In response, the show was extended until the end of December to accommodate the demand. But there were more significant changes on the horizon.

The first major change was that Jared Geller was demoted to associate producer despite the young producer's persistence in gaining Reubens' participation over a two-year period, while Reubens' friend Scott Sanders, who had recently scored a big Broadway hit with *The Color Purple*, was asked to serve as lead producer. Under Sanders' advisement, Alex Timbers was brought on to direct. Timbers was a young up-and-coming Broadway director with a

Pee-wee, Alex Timbers, and Scott Sanders at a press conference for *The Pee-wee Herman Show* in Los Angeles

© Lenora Claire

recent hit directing *Bloody Bloody Andrew Jackson.* Also on Sanders' advice, the show was relocated from the 1,300-seat venue to Club Nokia in downtown Los Angeles, with the ability to seat a thousand more, a move that also disrupted the show schedule, with the start date pushed back by two months.

Although Reubens and the producers maintained that the move was made in order to enable more fans to see the show, thousands of fans took to Pee-wee Herman's Facebook and Twitter pages to voice their displeasure about the move. On October 7, 2009, the *Los Angeles Times* reported that fans who had spent up to $1,500 in travel expenses to see the show now had to spend an additional $300 in cancellation fees after the dates were so drastically changed.

In response to the criticism, producer Scott Sanders says, "Paul called me and said, 'I think we're outgrowing the space.' As a producer, it felt clearer to me that it would be difficult, if not impossible, to make it work [at the Music Box]. It was a creative and artistic decision that evolved organically."

To apologize for the inconvenience, Sanders granted all original ticket holders a week to exchange their seats or receive a refund before tickets were made available to the general public (Music Box show ticketholders were given the best possible seat available at Club Nokia within the price range paid for the original ticket). Also, Reubens promised to treat all displaced customers to a half-hour question-and-answer session following each show.

Meanwhile, Reubens continued to work on the script with John Paragon and the show's original director Bill Steinkellner. On November 11, 2009, the actors reconvened for a second staged reading at Hollywood United Methodist Church. Within moments, it became clear that the show's changes were not limited to the performance venue and dates. There had been significant alterations in the script and cast since the first reading months earlier.

"The role of Sergio became a lot bigger," McGrath remembers. "There was a fantastic actor who played him [in the table reading]. I thought he was the best Latin actor by far of all who have played that role and its variations. Unfortunately, they replaced that actor, even though he had done all the readings."

To make the show more kid-friendly, Reubens omitted the more adult material from the original production and made the show similar to the children's series. As he did with converting the unused draft of *Pee-wee's Big Adventure* into *Pee-wee's Playhouse: The Movie*, Reubens added a number of *Playhouse* characters not present in the original live show. Many of the original cast were on standby expecting to reprise their roles, but found their characters' time on stage rapidly diminishing as the drafts progressed.

"Originally Paul asked Monica to do the musical salute because they weren't sure if I was available," says Brian Seff, who played Mr. Jelly Donut in the original production. "I emailed Paul and told him I was available, but once I saw the script, I just said to him I didn't see how it was going to work. In 1981 everyone still knew who Sly Stone was. I didn't know if audiences of today would get it."

In addition to fearing that some jokes would simply die, Seff had questions about the physical changes Reubens had undergone in the last several decades.

"I was surprised that Paul was doing it," he admits. "I wondered if he could still pull off that voice when he was fifty-seven years old."

As work on the script continued, the final form of the cast and crew started to take shape. Lynne Stewart and John Paragon were hired to reprise their roles as Miss Yvonne and Jambi the Genie from the original stage production and the television show, along with John Moody, who was a part of the original stage show as Mailman Mike. Groundling Phil LaMarr, from *MADtv* and *Pulp Fiction* fame, was tapped to fill in for Laurence Fishburne as Cowboy Curtis.

George McGrath and Alison Mork were hired to voice all of the puppets, but after the final staged reading, Reubens dropped a bomb on the two actors.

McGrath explains, "I was asked to do all of the table readings, and at the last one, I was told that I would be doing all of the male puppet voices offstage and Alison would do all the female ones. And then, right before rehearsals began, Paul said [Actors'] Equity wouldn't allow it — which meant that he'd tried to cut a deal to pay us less than scale and the union wouldn't go for it."

According to McGrath, Reubens claimed that hiring the two vocal actors would have cost him an extra $50,000. Instead, he intended to have the actors who played the human characters double as voices, a measure that would enable him to hire fewer people.

The producers rounded out the rest of the cast by hiring Josh Meyers to play Fireman Phineas, Jesse Garcia as Sergio, Drew Powell as Bear, and Lance Roberts as the King of Cartoons.

Gilbert Lewis and William Marshall had played the King of Cartoons for the television show (the latter passed away in 2003 from complications from Alzheimer's disease and diabetes). Lori Alan and Maceo Oliver were cast as understudies and puppet voices.

REBUILDING THE PLAYHOUSE

Most of the puppets were designed by Swazzle, a company based in Glendale, California. The group lobbied for the job after hearing word of Pee-wee's return to the stage.

Patrick Johnson of Swazzle rebuilds Randy

"We were good friends with Alison Mork and she mentioned to us that *The Pee-wee Herman Show* was starting up as a new live show," says Sean Johnson, co–creative director at Swazzle. "We figured they weren't going to dig the old puppets out of storage and thought we should be the ones to build new ones, so Alison passed our name along."

Despite having an insider-track to Reubens, it still took Swazzle some time to win the project. To help seal the deal, Johnson contacted the Chiodo Brothers, the production studio that had animated the Large Marge sequence in *Big Adventure*, and joined forces with them.

"It turned out the person in charge of hiring the puppet builders [for the new stage show] had done work with the Chiodos," Johnson says. "They were already being considered for the project. We just didn't know it."

Ultimately, both teams were brought on board to create the puppets. The Chiodo Brothers managed the project and contracted Swazzle to build 19 puppets and provide puppeteers for the show, while Alex in Wonderland, a company that specializes in costume-sized puppets, were brought on board to build Chairry and Conky.

Although Chairry had not been a part of the original stage production, Reubens knew that audiences would want to see their favorite character when the show was revived on stage in 2010. To make Chairry move, puppeteer Artie Esposito sat on a rolling chair with a built-in school desk, two other puppeteers would lower her shell over Esposito, and he would slip his arms into the sleeves of the puppet. Inside each of Chairry's arms were handles that controlled the mouth and eye movements.

"It was very comfortable," Esposito explains. "It was pretty much like an oversized costume where I got to sit the whole time."

Perhaps not *that* comfortable, since Chairry and Pee-wee shared a song-and-dance number that required Esposito to put his puppeteering skills to the test.

"It was heavy, but it was okay," Esposito recalls. "It was similar to when you sit in a chair and get stuck. When you stand up the chair is stuck on your butt. That's pretty much what it was like. When I would stand up to do the dance, the whole thing would come up with me and I would sort of waddle."

There were also some difficulties in translating the character from screen to stage. Alex Timbers stressed to the puppeteers the importance of the puppets looking alive at all times while on stage, an extra effort not required on the television series.

"That was the biggest challenge with Chairry," Esposito recalls. "Her part in the TV show was usually limited to one or two minutes of camera time and then Pee-wee would be in another part of the house. You didn't know what Chairry was doing. So I had to take Alison's movements and come up with other things for Chairry to do. Alison didn't do too much clapping, so I added that to the character. I had to add nuances I could keep up for ninety minutes so that when Chairry didn't have lines she wasn't dead."

The puppet builders at Swazzle also needed extra assistance to ensure that Pee-wee's talking fish remained physically active, even when they were not the center of attention.

© Swazzle Inc.

"The fish had a special motor that the Chiodo Brothers made that would keep them in perpetual motion," Johnson says. "Whenever necessary, a puppeteer would flip the motor off, have the fish say their lines, and then flip the switch back on."

Ever the problem-solvers, the Chiodos faced some big ones when it came to designing another *Playhouse* character.

"Magic Screen had to do on stage what she never had to do for the TV show, which is move by her own power," Sean Johnson explains.

To make her glide seamlessly in front of an audience, the Chiodo Brothers built a remote controlled puppet. The first Magic Screen was powered by a toy car that was weighed down to prevent her from zooming off stage.

"With that system there were also problems with the RC signals," says Victoria Johnson, who operated the puppet's body movements. "When Magic Screen would get close to Paul she would go berserk because of his wireless microphone."

In the week before its debut, the puppet was refitted with a new mechanism that enabled the Magic Screen to turn on a dime. The results made it easier for the puppeteers to control her and made for smoother, cleaner movements on stage. Unlike most of the puppets, Magic Screen was controlled by two puppeteers. While Victoria Johnson operated her body, Haley Jenkins operated her mouth. The duo had to work

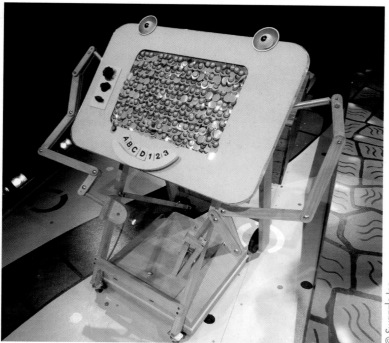

in sync with vocal actress Lori Alan to make the illusion work for the audience.

"As a puppeteer, you're used to doing the voice or using a prerecorded track," Victoria Johnson explains. "But it worked out. I think we executed it well."

While the puppeteers had many sessions of trial and error to get the characters to move fluidly, none posed a larger challenge than Pterri. To assist in his flight, the puppet received a facelift: his carved foam body was covered in neon lime green latex for maximum durability and mobility. Initially, the team had difficulty finding a way to move the puppet vertically through the stage space, but award-winning puppetry consultant Basil Twist suggested the group use a device called a split controller, which allowed the puppeteers to use horizontal space to make Pterri fly up and down.

Just as on the television show, more than one type of puppet was used to bring Pterri to life. A marionette puppet with a six-foot wingspan was used for when Pterri was in flight, and a hand puppet was used when vertical movement wasn't required. His size was expanded a few inches for maximum visibility in a large theater, with his height totaling two feet tall.

Joining fan favorites like Clocky, Conky, Globey, and Mr. Window on stage were two new characters. The team from Swazzle built Ginger, Cowboy Curtis's new anatomically correct mare who was designed by *Playhouse* puppet designer Wayne White, and Sham Wow, made of the hyper-absorbent hand towels made famous by late-night infomercials.

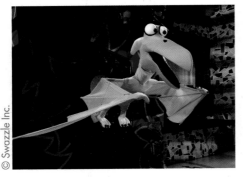

Testing an early version of Pterri at the Swazzle workshop and the finished puppet on stage

© Swazzle Inc.

As one might expect, the marionette Sham Wow puppet, designed by Patrick Johnson, was made of the actual product. There was even a phantasmal incarnation of the character from the Great Beyond — Ghost of Sham Wow.

Ghost of Sham Wow was born during an improvisational moment in rehearsal. Reubens jokingly threw Sham Wow into the deep-fat fryer during snack time and the cast immediately started rolling with a series of what-ifs: What if Sham Wow was now dead? What if the puppets all had a moment of silence? Reubens loved the suggestions and decided to integrate them into the scene, forgetting that the character had one more appearance later in the play. Several solutions were posed, like Sham Wow appearing burnt or deep-fried. But finally, someone suggested that he appear as a ghost.

"We called Ghost of Sham Wow 'old reliable,'" explains Carla Rudy, the puppeteer who operated the character. "No matter what else had happened with the marionettes that day, every time Ghost of Sham Wow popped down, he always killed. The audience loved it."

Despite the conventional wisdom, Ghost of Sham Wow designer Artie Esposito recalls that the character struck a particularly strong chord with children.

"Paul thought that kids were going to be afraid of Ghost Wow," Esposito says. "But when he would go do the Q&A, kids would always say Ghost of Sham Wow was their favorite part of the show."

According to Esposito, Reubens was surprised that kids really enjoyed characters from a horror genre, and has an idea for a kids show involving ghosts and monsters, which might leave the door open for Ghost of Sham Wow to rise again from the dead.

As fun as it was to create the new characters, the team at Swazzle was disappointed when the Puppetland Band was removed from the show weeks before opening.

"It's funny because we had all picked which ones we were going to build," Esposito recalls. "Then the day we came in to start building, we got the phone call that they were being taken off the table."

A number of factors caused the characters to be cut from the show.

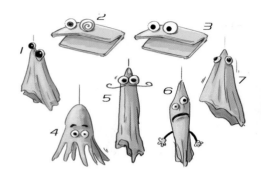

Patrick Johnson's Sham Wow design and the finished puppets

"Paul mentioned many times that the budget was about two million dollars, which sounds like a lot, but is still a finite amount of money," Sean Johnson explains. "The puppets were bid at a price that made them unaffordable, unfortunately."

In addition to the cost, the physical limitations of Club Nokia might have played a role.

"The puppets were supposed to roll out on a giant platform that was a huge set piece," Johnson says. "It was also going to require three more puppeteers to get into that area."

The most significant reason the characters were cut was the mature content of their scenes. While the show definitely employed suggestive humor that would have been over the heads of most children, the sequences involving the Puppetland Band were surprisingly risqué.

In a November 2009 draft of the script, the Puppetland Band appears on stage "laughing hysterically amid a cloud of smoke." It's discovered that Chicky Baby had just scored some medical marijuana and the group tries to get Pee-wee to take a hit from an oversized bong because he often seems anxious. Pee-wee is tempted, but ultimately decides to pass.

"I have the type of personality where I'd go right to heroin," Pee-wee says.

With the new puppets ready for their stage debut and the cast in place, *The Pee-wee Herman Show* was ready to return. For the team at Swazzle, working on the project that called for them to recreate some of their favorite childhood characters was a once-in-a-lifetime experience.

"Like a lot of people, we grew up watching *Pee-wee's Playhouse*," Sean Johnson explains. "We used to watch the show and annoy our parents by screaming whenever someone said the secret word. So, to work on this show was amazing. It's so boring to say it was a dream come true, but it really was."

The Swazzle puppeteers in rehearsals

PEE-WEE LEARNS TO FLY

On Tuesday, January 12, 2010, a sold-out audience of thousands packed into Club Nokia, many with Pee-wee Herman dolls in hand and red bowties around their necks. For those who grew up watching *Pee-wee's Playhouse* in the 1980s, this was the must-see event of the year, and everyone approaching the venue could sense the anticipation and excitement in the air.

As the crowd gathered inside, the cast and crew prepared for the show ahead, the culmination of many sleepless nights and long rehearsals during the day. For those who had been involved in the original show, this night marked what they hoped would be a triumphant return to a concept that had been developed nearly 30 years earlier. If they were lucky, it would be a testament to all the hard work and dedication they had shown in the early '80s to create an

event that would transcend the small Groundling Theatre and become an internationally recognized phenomenon. As the cast and crew, new and old, huddled together before the show, everyone hoped for the best and waited for the unknown.

As showtime neared, they all took their places backstage. Puppeteers Carla Rudy and Erik Kuska took their places near one of the video monitors behind the set and thus experienced the first seconds of Pee-wee's return firsthand.

"I had done tons of shows and thought this was a cool gig, but that was initially all I thought of it," Rudy says. "But when it was the first performance and Pee-wee walked out against the curtain in that lone spotlight, it was like a rock concert. There were cheers upon cheers and it didn't stop. That experience just brought tears to our eyes. It affects you in such a deeply profound way, and that's when I understood how important this show was to so many people."

Kuska, who also grew up watching *Pee-wee's Playhouse*, shares his sentiments.

"We didn't realize it at first, but that wave of applause and love started twenty-five years ago," he says. "When Pee-wee went away, we all just went about our lives holding it in, but finally there was a chance to have that release opening night and it repeated every performance. Each audience had their own moment to go back to when they were on the living room floor watching Pee-wee, yelling, and eating Cap'n Crunch cereal. It was just amazing to experience that."

As with the children's show, the reaction was mixed among those who worked on the original production and had received complimentary tickets from Paul for the new production. Monica Ganas, who played Mrs. Jelly Donut in 1981 cast, was pleased with the show.

"What struck me was how different it was from other shows currently out there," she said. "Everybody left with this big grin on their faces." For Ganas, the experience of seeing a show she had once been in was unique.

"The show was different enough where it didn't feel like déjà vu," she says. "But there was a kind of sentimental aspect to seeing it."

For Dawna Kaufmann, who had first approached Reubens with the idea of doing a live kiddie-show for adults, the experience at Club Nokia was a disappointment.

"When we did the show, we charged people ten dollars to get in," she says. "They did the same show that we did at the Groundling, with a couple of little changes, and charged people a hundred and twenty-five

Fan Ariel Eby meets Pee-wee after *The Pee-wee Herman Show*

© Swazzle Inc.

dollars to see it. It was lazy. When you increase the ticket prices and charge people twenty-five dollars to park, you have a commitment to give people one hell of a show. Paul just didn't do that."

Nonetheless, the Club Nokia engagement was considered a rousing success and earned rave reviews from *Entertainment Weekly*, *Variety*, and the *Hollywood Reporter*, which paved the way for a comeback that can only be described as anything but pee-wee in size. After watching the final matinee performance with his wife, Hollywood funnyman Judd Apatow, the director of *Knocked Up* and *The 40-Year-Old Virgin*, spoke to Reubens about the possibility of bringing Pee-wee Herman back to the big screen.

"He told me that he had never seen his wife laugh so hard before," Reubens says. "I think that convinced him to approach me to do this."

Reubens already had two scripts lying in wait, but Apatow hired a young writer named Paul Rust to cowrite a new script with the actor that would see Pee-wee embarking on a road-trip adventure. Even though his other scripts have been once again put on the backburner, Reubens and his long list of collaborators remain hopeful that *Pee-wee's Playhouse: The Movie* will find its way to theaters eventually.

According to Reubens, Chris Rock, a documented *Big Adventure* fan, has given his word that he will play the villainous El Chunky Boobabi if the film gets made. During a 2006 *Entertainment Weekly* interview, Laurence Fishburne and S. Epatha Merkerson — who played Cowboy Curtis and Reba the Mail Lady, respectively — expressed interest in reprising their roles in a *Playhouse* film. Suzanne Kent, who played Mrs. Rene, would also be interested in appearing, if the opportunity came around.

"Paul spoke about the movie to me a while ago," Kent says, "but I haven't asked him about it since. I trust that he knows what I can do. He knows who I am. He knows my

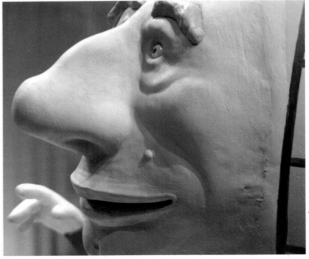

© Swazzle Inc.

talent and I'm sure that if I'm needed, he will let me know."

Playhouse animator Kent Burton also hopes his services are needed for a *Playhouse* film and that the dinosaur family would be included.

"A *Playhouse* film would be perfect because if you have ninety minutes to play with, there could be three dinosaur bits instead of one," Burton says. "So, I have my fingers crossed."

Of course, a film that takes the puppet characters out of the playhouse would provide an opportunity for their operators to come back as well.

"If we're so lucky, we'll be a part of the movie," Sean Johnson says. "And hopefully we'll be working alongside Alison Mork and Kevin Carlson and the originals from the TV show, too."

For Mork, a spot in a *Playhouse* film may be all but guaranteed.

"When Paul let Alison and I know we weren't going to be a part of the stage show, he gave us his personal guarantee that we would be in the *Playhouse* movie," George McGrath says.

At the time of writing, production on *Pee-wee's Playhouse: The Movie* has once again reached a standstill, but Suzanne Kent is confident that the film will see the light of day.

"Paul has always been the kind of guy that makes whatever project he wants to do happen," she says. "It may not be exactly when he wants, but it will happen."

On May 20, 2010, it was announced that *The Pee-wee Herman Show* would be heading

to Broadway for a six-week engagement at the new Stephen Sondheim Theatre on West 43rd Street. The news ended months of speculation among Pee-wee fans that the show might tour the country or even take up residency in Las Vegas. Most of the show's Los Angeles cast was rehired for the New York run, but Lori Alan was unable to make the move and so she was replaced by Lexy Fridell. With the exception of Haley Jenkins, the entire Swazzle team was replaced by local puppeteers.

In the weeks before the Broadway run, Reubens went on a media publicity blitz. He reminisced about *Pee-wee's Playhouse Christmas Special* with Whoopi Goldberg on *The View*; reenacted the *Big Adventure* Large Marge sequence and was interviewed while riding a bicycle on *Late Night with Jimmy Fallon*; conducted the world's largest Tequila dance from Sturgis,

South Dakota, on a taped segment of *The Tonight Show with Jay Leno*; and took a tour of Manhattan with Regis Philbin, who wore a matching Pee-wee suit. Once, the idea of a comeback for Paul Reubens had seemed farfetched to say the least, but now it was obvious that Reubens had rewritten the ending of Pee-wee's story into a happy one.

In the cold evening of October 26, 2010, three generations of Pee-wee fans filed into the Stephen Sondheim Theatre to witness the Broadway debut. As some checked out the new merchandise, others headed to the bar for a pre-show alcoholic beverage, a marked departure from the juice boxes they'd consumed while watching Pee-wee decades earlier.

Finally, the audience moved into the auditorium and took their seats. As the lights dimmed in the theater to signal that the show was starting,

Fan Christina Henriquez approaches the Stephen Sondheim Theatre to watch *The Pee-wee Herman Show*

a hush fell over the crowd, and then, as the lone spotlight hit the curtain, the crowd erupted into applause that only grew more frenzied when Pee-wee emerged from behind the curtain and stepped into the light. His first few lines were inaudible as the crowd screamed, whistled, and many chanted, "Pee-wee! Pee-wee! Pee-wee!"

This scene repeated throughout the evening, with fits of madness taking over otherwise mature adults when Miss Yvonne, Cowboy Curtis, and Jambi each appeared on stage for the first time. At the declaration of the secret word, which was "fun," the crowd screamed even before they were told to, and throughout the 90-minute show no one missed a chance to let their inner-child exclaim whenever the secret word was said.

In *The Pee-wee Herman Show*'s final minutes, the stage lights surged as Miss Yvonne, Cowboy Curtis, Sergio the Repairman, Fireman Phineas, Mailman Mike, the King of Cartoons, a man dressed in a bear mascot suit, and over a dozen puppets joined Jambi the Genie in repeating the magic words — *mekka lekka hi mekka hiney ho, mekka lekka hi mekka hiney ho, mekka lekka hi mekka hiney ho*. Before they were prompted, the congregation of over a thousand enthusiastic devotees joined in the methodical chant. Within moments, the stage went completely dark, with occasional flashes of lightening created by two large strobe lights built into the stage and loud thunderclaps controlled by a soundboard in the rear of the Broadway playhouse.

"It's working, it's working!" Jambi exclaimed. "Everyone in the audience repeat after me. *Mekka lekka hi mekka hiney ho*."

The group of former Saturday morning spectators of Pee-wee's world was now an integral component in making their hero's wish to fly come true. At first, the words were interspersed with giggles from the sold-out crowd, but by the third repetition, the chant reverberated with strength and deliberation throughout the theater. *Mekka lekka hi mekka hiney ho, mekka lekka hi mekka hiney ho!*

Within moments, Pee-wee's familiar nasal cry voice pierced the darkness as a spotlight slowly illuminated his body, which appeared to be in mid-flight with the assistance of expensive machinery, special lighting, and a puppet body. The onlookers laughed, applauded, and "screamed real loud" with excitement.

"I'm Pee-wee Herman," he said. "I'm the luckiest boy in the world."

With that, he waved goodbye to the boys and girls of varying ages and

Fan Rob Michael Hugel meets Pee-wee in New York

continued his flight off stage, leaving the audience behind just as he had at the end of his original live production, at the end of *Pee-wee's Big Adventure*, in the opening dream sequence of *Big Top Pee-wee*, at the end of every *Playhouse* episode, and before his decades-long hiatus.

The audience began applauding wildly. As the sound grew, an elementary school–aged boy jumped out of his seat and turned his head to try and catch a last glimpse of the flying 58-year-old man who seems perennially ageless. He asked a woman sitting next to him where Pee-wee was going.

The woman, who wore a vintage black-and-white sweatshirt emblazoned with a cartoon headshot of Pee-wee, looked back at her young escort. She handed him the pull-string doll dressed in a gray suit she was holding and leaned forward to pick up the bag of merchandise she had purchased in the lobby before the show began.

"He'll be back," she said as the boy extended his arm to make the doll fly through the air. "Pee-wee Herman isn't going anywhere."

7 | APPRAISING THE PLAYHOUSE

WHILE *PEE-WEE'S PLAYHOUSE* was an undeniable television phenomenon during the show's run, the task of developing a children's show out of a late-night live production for adults required a measure of brazenness. The concept was original, but as any seasoned television executive will tell you, originality doesn't always lead to success.

© Ken Sax

"When Judy Price green-lit the show, we all told her we knew it was going to be a hit," says Steve Oakes, supervising producer of the first season. "She just sort of rolled her eyes and said, 'Guys, I love what you're doing, but I wish I knew which shows were going to be a hit. How about you do your best and we'll see?'"

Much to Price's delight, Oakes' instincts were correct — the show was a hit. While many had accurately predicted the show would be a success, several others involved with the show's first season harbored doubts about whether it would resonate with the public.

"I have to confess," says animation director Phil Trumbo. "When edits were being put together of the show, I'd see some of them and think, 'Wow, this is just too weird. It's just too funky, it's just too loose.' I didn't know if anyone was going to get it."

However, within a few weeks of the show's debut, millions of viewers had "got it." For some, the visuals were enough to captivate their attention. Others found themselves laughing at the show's mature yet childlike sense of humor. However, for many, *Playhouse* was worth watching simply for the host himself, a blank slate onto which people projected their

perceptions of what either an uninhibited adult or physically overdeveloped child could be if he had enough money to furnish his own playhouse to his heart's desire.

Pee-wee Herman is a truly polarizing character, and people find him to be either hilarious or irritating, depending on their vantage point. He's virtually impossible to just like. You either love him or hate him. This was true during the time of the show's run and continues to be today.

"Over the years I have gotten a lot of unsolicited opinions on Pee-wee," says writer George McGrath. "When the show aired on Adult Swim, there was a violent reaction against him from their target audience, teenage boys. The stuff they wrote on the Cartoon Network website was surprisingly hateful. At the same time, I put the theme song on YouTube a few years ago and get comments almost every day, with most of the positive ones about warm childhood memories of watching the show. The negative ones are not about the show so much as they are about Paul."

It's difficult to pinpont what caused *Pee-wee's Playhouse* to leave an indelible imprint on our popular culture. When questioned in interviews, Paul Reubens declines to analyze the show's success, and he leaves that responsibility to others. To that end, here is what several people involved in the show's production have said about why Pee-wee Herman and his play-house have stood the test of time in our shared consciousness.

Gary Austin, founder of the Groundlings: "I imagine the strongest group of people still interested is adults who were kids during the *Playhouse* years. I have a good friend who was a kid during that time and is desperately hoping that I can find a way for him and Paul to meet. Our heroes make such an impact and we carry that with us throughout our lives."

Steve Binder, producer of the second and third season of *Pee-wee's Playhouse* and *Pee-wee's Playhouse Christmas Special*: "The quality speaks for itself. The episodes are funny. It was a great discovery when the programmers of children's television learned that they didn't need to order sixty-five episodes of a show. Kids wanted to see their favorite episodes over and over again. The *Playhouse* will always attract an audience with the original episodes that were produced. They're funny and smart. Many shows are dated because of the material or the costumes, but that's not a problem with Pee-wee."

Kent Burton, animator for the first, fourth, and fifth seasons of *Pee-wee's Playhouse*: "Whenever someone finds out I worked this show, they say to me, 'You know, that was the only time I ever got up early on Saturday morning,' and I'm talking about grown-up people with families. I've heard that so many times I can't count them all. 'I used to set the alarm for that show.' I think the show's remained

Kent Burton animates the Dinosaur Family

popular because it has such a wide range. I mean, it could go in any direction. Think about the humor. Paul had a way of being childish, but at the same time, a lot of his humor was made for adults. It was edgy and not always politically correct. They could pull some things and not really be insulting, even though in some ways it was, because it was done in such a kid's style."

Johann Carlo and Pee-wee

Johann Carlo, Dixie on the first season of *Pee-wee's Playhouse*: "I think Paul hit on something very primal. We all have a kid inside us and, because of that, the show was so personal. There's that old cliché about the more personal something is, the more universal it is. We could all relate to it and imagine how much fun it would be to step into Pee-wee's shoes. He's the king of his domain and has all of his guests. We all want to have a playhouse where we're in charge and can do whatever we wanted. There was no adult supervision. The adults like Miss Yvonne were all like kids. When you're young, all you want is to be a grown-up, but you still want to be a kid. *Pee-wee's Playhouse* was a whole world just like that."

© Ken Sax

Scott Chester, associate producer for the first season of *Pee-wee's Playhouse* **and** *Big Top Pee-wee* **and personal assistant to Paul Reubens from 1987 to 1988:** "People ask me all the time if I think we could make *Pee-wee's Playhouse* now and my answer is always no. They'd make you use computers and wouldn't allow us to have the freedom to do time-extensive, expensive animation. The animation would probably be outsourced to a company overseas and it wouldn't have the originality that we had."

Dave Daniels, animator for all five seasons of *Pee-wee's Playhouse*: "The show still resonates because it was an interesting, free-form collage of very eclectic stuff that was somehow held together by Paul Reubens' personality and character. As an artistic piece, it wasn't confining. There was always something original or weird right around the corner, and it didn't fall apart. A lot of shows that try to do that fail because they don't have enough of a through-line that holds the audience together, or because the separate pieces aren't all energetic enough, but the show's producers found a way to unleash all this creativity in lots of individuals. I'm surprised that formula hasn't been pulled off again."

Prudence Fenton, animation and effects producer for all five seasons of *Pee-wee's Playhouse* **and 1986 Daytime Emmy Award winner for producing the show's opening titles:** "It was such an amazing, creative experience. The whole message of the show and all the images and the design were perfect. When I would work on commercials during the hiatuses of the show, I can't tell you how many times I'd walk into an agency and they'd say, 'Okay, we're looking for something really hip and cool like *Pee-wee's Playhouse*.' It really left its mark on the culture. Creatively it just opened tons of doors."

Monica Ganas, Mrs. Jelly Donut in the 1981 production of *The Pee-wee Herman Show*: "There's something more timeless about the show than anyone could have imagined and I think it's because of all the artistry in it. Artful material holds up, period. What I love about Pee-wee is that he doesn't edit anything. He comes right out and says what people wouldn't dare say. He's a perfect example of how we really are, not how we pretend to be. To have a character that does that for us in one minute, and in the next minute be showing us big underwear and making us laugh, is so truthful. No matter what any character does on that show, no one is above being forgiven and accepted back into the family. Nobody gives up on anybody."

Troy Hughes-Palmer, animator for seasons four and five of *Pee-wee's Playhouse*: "The show's lasting success probably has more to do with Paul and his artistic vision than anything else. His lasting appeal probably speaks more of his vision as an artist than anything."

Vaughn Tyree Jelks, Fabian of the Playhouse Gang on the second season of *Pee-wee's Playhouse*: "The show had that sense of fantasy we all love. It took us to a world where chairs can talk and grown men can have a timeless quality about them. It stuck around because of that. Pee-wee meant a lot of different things to different people. When I was thirteen, the set intrigued me, but to older people who knew him from his movies, he meant something different. You'd be watching the same guy, but having a different experience and I think that's one of the reasons why Paul Reubens has worked for so long. It's kind of like *Sesame Street*, but on a more mature level. It appeals to adults just as much as it does to kids."

Dawna Kaufmann, executive in charge of production of the 1981 production of *The Pee-wee Herman Show*: "I'm not surprised the concept, in its various formations, has endured for three decades. Give an audience a colorful environment, actors who are fun to watch, and quick-moving story lines that seem naughty yet familiar, and it's a pretty solid bet for success."

Suzanne Kent, Mrs. Rene from the second through fifth seasons of *Pee-wee's Playhouse*: "It was ahead of its time. The show was just fun and colorful and wacky and it appeals to grown-ups in grown-up ways and it appeals to kids in kid ways. It's a great cross-section. Sometimes the kids don't understand exactly what the grown-ups understand and sometimes the grown-ups don't understand exactly what the kids understand because of the ways the jokes are played out. The writing was ingenious like that. The show clicks with any age group during any time; when we did it in the late '80s, early '90s, up until today. It's never dated."

Pee-wee and Suzanne Kent

John Duke Kisch, still photographer for the first season of *Pee-wee's Playhouse*: "It's unique. It makes you smile. He's a great character and we need that in our lives. You know, there aren't a lot of great characters in our history, but the ones that last are endearing. For those of us who were a part of it, the show remains on the top shelf of our hearts, but for those who are complete fans from watching on TV, he's of this upper-echelon of greatness that will live on forever."

Glenn Lazzaro, animation editor for the first season of *Pee-wee's Playhouse*: "The man-child thing was absolutely brilliant. That idea that when you're a child you can get away with anything, you can dream anything, almost like a cartoon character. There was so much adult content in it, but he was still a sort-of child saying these sarcastic and ironic things. He had this innocence that made you wish you were that smart when you were a kid."

Steve Oakes, supervising coproducer of the first season of *Pee-wee's Playhouse*: "*Pee-wee's Playhouse* has had its imitators, but none have stepped up to move beyond what was accomplished. It was a pretty unique coming together of talent that transcended a kids' entertainment show to be grounded in an aesthetic that goes deeper into our cultural mix of references. I'm not saying the show is high art, but it ended up having staked out some territory that was pretty unique."

Steve Oakes

Wayne Orr, codirector with Paul Reubens on the second season of *Pee-wee's Playhouse* and *Pee-wee's Christmas Special*: "The show is charming. It's not hateful. Some of children's television today is very low-brow, but there were so many bright things that went on in *Pee-wee's Playhouse*. There's nothing in the show that can be taken as hateful or nasty in any way. Somebody might be the butt of a joke or something once in a while, but it's never anything that lingers, and people certainly didn't hold grudges. I don't know how many times I've had people tell me their whole fraternity would get around the TV on Saturday morning and watch *Pee-wee's Playhouse*. The show speaks to people if they're young, or even if they are a little older, because there were things in there for older people, fun things that the kids weren't going to get, but their older brothers or their fathers or mothers would. We never talked down to people and weren't overly concerned about making sure the episodes played well with kids. We knew they would, and that if we did our jobs, everybody will enjoy it."

© John Duke Kisch / CBS

Judy Price, vice president of children's programming at CBS during the time *Pee-wee's Playhouse* **was on air:** "There's something special about the character. Believe me, if we could have captured and bottled it, we would have done so a long time ago. There are characters that come along that just have that ingredient. He's engaging, he's charming, he's childlike, and he's innocent. It's a combination that works and is very effective. It stands the test of time. If you look across the canon of classic characters, whether from literature or cinema or television, there are some that just stand the test of time and Pee-wee Herman is one of them. He's got a dose of nostalgia. He's like Peter Pan. He takes us off into another world of imagination."

Ken Sax, still photographer for the second season of *Pee-wee's Playhouse*: "Paul was definitely a genius. To come up with such an ensemble show like that, you've got to be a genius. It was epic."

Phil Trumbo, animation director for the first season of *Pee-wee's Playhouse* **and 1986 Daytime Emmy Award winner for directing the show's opening titles:** "What's really cool is to have been involved with something that has touched so many generations, an entertainment property that's so iconic. When the DVDs came out, Paul sent me a complimentary set, which was very nice. My daughter, who'd never even seen the show, was suddenly watching them and running around screaming the secret word. The show is classic."

Michael Chase Walker, west coast director of children's programs at CBS during the time *Pee-wee's Playhouse* **was on air:** "Essentially you have a character in contrast. You have a dichotomous character embodied in one figure, the boy-man, and it's probably one of the greatest archetypes in comedy. Whether it's Charlie Chaplin in *The Kid* or Laurel and Hardy,

John Paragon turns into Jambi in 1981, 1986, and 2010

they're physical men as innocent, foolish characters where they encounter things with childlike reactions and innocence. How many of us are boy-men? We have these bodies and these jobs and so much is expected of us, but we constantly fuck up in our jobs and with our girlfriends and don't always have the wherewithal and maturity to handle things in a proper way. Pee-wee is no exception. He has this wonderment about sexuality, girls, toys, and he represents that Peter Pan quality that is a part of all of us."

Stephanie Walski, Rapunzel of the Playhouse Gang on the second season of *Pee-wee's Playhouse*: "*Pee-wee's Playhouse* was something that will never be replicated. It was such a breakthrough show. It used these old kid's shows as a jumping-off point and took those concepts to an entirely different level. They haven't been able to recreate it, nor do I think they ever will. Its staying power and popularity speaks to how magical and educational the show was. It was literally a child's imagination come to life."

152

© John Duke Kisch / CBS

SEASON 1

1986–1987

1.01 • ICE CREAM SOUP

Written by: George McGrath, John Paragon, Paul Reubens, Max Robert, and Michael Varhol
Directed by: Stephen R. Johnson
Original airdate: September 13, 1986

© John Duke Kisch / CBS

THE INAUGURAL EPISODE of the series finds Pee-wee establishing some of the features that came to define the series, including connect-the-dots, the secret word of the day, and snack time. Pee-wee makes ice cream soup by putting ice cream in a bowl and mixing it with chocolate syrup, but Randy ruins the snack by throwing off the chocolate-to-vanilla ratio. Pee-wee and his friends solve the problem by adding more ice cream.

While the episode is low on plot, "Ice Cream Soup" has a pretty high dosage of fun. Captain Carl's adventure through the Sandwich Islands is great to watch, especially with Phil Hartman's stellar commitment to character as buckets of water crash against his face. Although the episode is put together well, it becomes obviously a pilot when Pee-wee uses his wish to ensure that everyone tunes in for next week's episode. There's no better way to ensure good ratings than to have a genie pull some strings. Although I always thought ice cream soup was made by just letting it melt in your bowl, I credit this episode for teaching me the *real* recipe.

The Secret Word of the Day: Door
The King's Cartoon: *The Fresh Vegetable Mystery* (produced by Fleisher Studios in 1939)
Blink and You'll Miss: Check out the Frankenstein doll in Pee-wee's toy collection. Look familiar? It's similar to the kinds of toys made by Sid, the destructive kid in *Toy Story*.

1.02 • LUAU FOR TWO

Written by: George McGrath, John Paragon, Paul Reubens, Max Robert, and Michael Varhol
Directed by: Stephen R. Johnson
Original airdate: September 20, 1986

AFTER WINNING A Hawaiian dinner for two from a television game show, Pee-wee faces the tough decision of who to take with him. Over the course of the day, nearly every one of his pals attempts to brown-nose him into being his guest. With the help of Randy, Pee-wee gets wise to everyone's faux acts of kindness and reprimands them for trying to use him. Jambi rectifies the situation by having a luau in the playhouse that everyone can join.

© George McGrath

"Luau for Two" is an excellent episode, especially with Captain Carl's declaration that "there's nothing [he] wouldn't do for a platter of pupu." Watching the characters lobby for Pee-wee's plus-one is truly entertaining, as is the loose shooting style of the final party sequence. The episode's lesson, where Pee-wee instructs those in the viewing audience to not betray their good friends, makes this episode worthwhile. It's a valuable moral delivered in pure Pee-wee Herman style.

The Secret Word of the Day: Fun
The King's Cartoon: *Ants in the Plants* (produced by Fleisher Studios in 1940)
Fun Fact: This episode marks the only appearance of the talking Comedy and Tragedy masks.
You May Remember: Pee-wee covers his face with scotch tape, just as he did during his morning routine in *Pee-wee's Big Adventure*. Also, fanatics may notice this episode's secret word was recycled for the 2010 revival of *The Pee-wee Herman Show*.
Blink and You'll Miss: Miss Yvonne isn't only the most beautiful woman in Puppetland; she's also the thriftiest! She wears the same blue dress from the pilot episode. Also, the wacky camera angles during the luau enable you to see the top edges of the playhouse set and the stage equipment high above.

1.03 • RAINY DAY

Written by: George McGrath, John Paragon, Paul Reubens, Max Robert, and Michael Varhol
Directed by: Stephen R. Johnson
Original airdate: September 27, 1986

WHEN PEE-WEE'S PLANS get derailed by the weather, he and his pals demonstrate how to have fun on a rainy day. By camping indoors, telling ghost stories, and making hot chocolate, they make the most of what could have been a gloomy day.

© John Duke Kisch / CBS

While the episode's plot sounds thin, it is actually quite entertaining. Reba makes her first appearance in the series and the prank-calling sequence is a true delight to watch. In a twenty-first century age of Skype and video-conferencing, this episode serves as a reminder of how forward-thinking the *Playhouse* creative team was for their picture phone idea. The episode also wins bonus points for being practical. What child doesn't need some tips to have fun when the weather outside is frightful?

The Secret Word of the Day: Help
The King's Cartoon: *Summertime* (produced by Ub Iwerks in 1935)
Fun Fact: Pee-wee's "shaving just like daddy" bit was also part of his standup routine in the early 1980s.
You May Remember: When the lights go out in the playhouse, the animation is similar to the scene in *Pee-wee's Big Adventure* when Pee-wee uses his headlight glasses. With the assistance of clever puppetry, this same gag was included in the Broadway run of *The Pee-wee Herman Show*.
Blink and You'll Miss: The secret word appears in red during the whipped cream explosion, marking the only time it appears a different color. Also, if you blink during the end credits, you might not realize that the couple Randy and Pee-wee prank call is series puppeteers Alison Mork and George McGrath.

1.04 • NOW YOU SEE ME, NOW YOU DON'T

Written by: George McGrath, John Paragon, Paul Reubens, Max Robert, and Michael Varhol
Directed by: Stephen R. Johnson
Original airdate: October 4, 1986

PEE-WEE USES A magic kit to produce a show for his friends that ends up making him disappear. He enjoys his time as an invisible body, but panics when he realizes that to make himself reappear he has to purchase another magic kit and wait several weeks for it to be delivered. Before the episode's end, Jambi makes Pee-wee's body visible again.

This episode stands out for its show-within-a-show plotline, especially with all of the magic tricks that go wrong, and is reminiscent of old *Our Gang* comedies. The failed magic act sequence adds an air of charm to the episode and also offers some glimpses of Pee-wee Herman's origin as a bad standup comedian. The sheer number of *Playhouse* characters present in this episode provide another reason for you to give this one a watch. Despite the episode's charm, the writers lose a point for missing an obvious joke. When Pee-wee lifts Miss Yvonne's dress and says, "I see London, I see France," Globey could have said, "They're over here!"

Ric Heitzman and Globey

The Secret Word of the Day: Little
The King's Cartoon: *Smile, Darn Ya, Smile!* (produced by Rudolf Ising in 1931)
You May Remember: Pee-wee's foil ball was a routine part of the 1981 and 2010 productions of *The Pee-wee Herman Show.*
Blink and You'll Miss: Pee-wee's name appears misspelled twice. On the card advertising his magic show, the hyphen is missing. Then later, when his name appears on the Magic Screen, the hyphen is missing again and the "w" is capitalized.

1.05 • JUST ANOTHER DAY

Written by: George McGrath, John Paragon, Paul Reubens, Max Robert, and Michael Varhol
Directed by: Stephen R. Johnson
Original airdate: October 11, 1986

© John Duke Kisch / CBS

COWBOY CURTIS TEACHES Pee-wee how to square dance and Pee-wee reciprocates by teaching Cowboy Curtis how to pogo, which involves jumping up and down to rock music while wearing a Mohawk wig. With the help of some clever animation, Pee-wee invites the audience at home to see inside his head, while his brain rests in an easy chair. The episode continues on a series of random yet funny vignettes.

As the title suggests, "Just Another Day" is light on plot, but it is pretty impressive when it comes to memorable sequences. This is one episode that parents might have wanted to shield their children from, simply due to the amount of loud and crazy things kids might be inspired to do as a result of watching. The sight of Pee-wee and Cowboy Curtis pogo dancing is extremely funny, especially with the bright wigs the two wear. There's nothing that screams '80s more than the sight of Pee-wee Herman jumping around in a mosh-pit with a vibrantly colored punk wig on. As fun as this episode must have been for children watching, one can almost imagine parents collectively covering their ears when, at the end of the episode, Pee-wee instructs the viewing audience to get "anything that makes noise" and start banging loudly.

The Secret Word of the Day: Back
The King's Cartoon: *Old Mother Hubbard* (produced by Ub Iwerks in 1935)
Fun Fact: Although he is not credited, Dog Chair is portrayed in this episode by George McGrath.
Bet You Didn't Know: When this episode was released on VHS by MGM/UA in 1996, the title was inexplicably changed to "Cowboy Fun." The 2004 Image Entertainment DVD release reinstated the proper title.
Blink and You'll Miss: We learn that Mr. Kite is married, though we never meet Mrs. Kite. They are the only married puppet characters.

1.06 • BEAUTY MAKEOVER

Written by: George McGrath, John Paragon, Paul Reubens, Max Robert, and Michael Varhol
Directed by: Stephen R. Johnson
Original airdate: October 18, 1986

MISS YVONNE GIVES Mrs. Steve a makeover, which Pee-wee expects to be disastrous. After a lengthy process, Mrs. Steve is revealed to be physically unchanged, but leaves the playhouse happy. Miss Yvonne tells Pee-wee, and the viewing audience, that Mrs. Steve was happy because she feels beautiful, "and when you feel beautiful, you are beautiful."

This episode is arguably the best from the show's first season. It's great to see an episode centered on Mrs. Steve, and Shirley Stoler shines. The episode scores extra points for producing the most genuine laughs from the viewing audience during the show's first season. When Pee-wee falls on the ground laughing after finding out Mrs. Steve is the recipient of Miss Yvonne's makeover offer, it is impossible to not do the same at home. Go ahead;:watch it and tell me you didn't laugh. Finally, this episode earns extremely high marks for hitting home one of the show's central themes: you should be tolerant of everyone regardless of how they look and who they are.

Miss Yvonne, Mrs. Steve, and Pee-wee with Sid Bartholomew

The Secret Word of the Day: Time
The King's Cartoon: *Goldilocks and the Three Bears* (produced by Ub Iwerks in 1935)
Blink and You'll Miss: Some of Martin Denny's sound effects from the opening titles turn up in the dinosaur sequence — although, I suppose this really is more of a "cover your ears and you'll miss it" sort of thing!

1.07 • THE RESTAURANT

Written by: George McGrath, John Paragon, Paul Reubens, Max Robert, and Michael Varhol
Directed by: Stephen R. Johnson
Original airdate: October 25, 1986

© John Duke Kisch / CBS

CAPTAIN CARL AND Pee-wee pretend the playhouse is a restaurant. After Carl orders a steak, Pee-wee informs him that the only thing on the menu is a very expensive peanut butter and jelly sandwich. Carl gets annoyed and takes off. Later on, Tito comes over and, with the help of Conky, teaches Pee-wee about scuba diving in the ocean.

"The Restaurant" really shines during the underwater sequence at the end, and during the restaurant scene with Captain Carl. Phil Hartman's character is at his best when he grows frustrated with Pee-wee's antics. Captain Carl and Pee-wee share their best scene together during the whole series' run. Even though the character only appears in a few *Playhouse* episodes, "The Restaurant" shows just why he's remembered so fondly among Pee-wee fans. While it is fun to watch, Hartman's scene serves as an unfortunate reminder of talent that was gone too soon.

The Secret Word of the Day: Day
The King's Cartoon: *Molly Moo-Cow and the Butterflies* (produced by Burt Gillett and Tom Palmer in 1935)
You May Remember: The temper tantrum Pee-wee throws after wasting his wish is reminiscent of the fit he has during the original *Pee-wee Herman Show*.
Blink and You'll Miss: As Pee-wee and Tito swim underwater, they forget one important piece of equipment — the scuba gear!

1.08 • ANTS IN YOUR PANTS

Written by: George McGrath, John Paragon, Paul Reubens, Max Robert, and Michael Varhol
Directed by: Stephen R. Johnson
Original airdate: November 1, 1986

PEE-WEE AND the Playhouse Gang notice the ants have escaped from their farm and are wreaking havoc all over the playhouse. Thankfully, Jambi uses his powers to return them to their container. Later in the episode, Conky detects smoke and Pee-wee sets off to extinguish the fire. It's discovered to be Randy, with a cigarette in his hand, because he believes "smoking makes you look cool." Pee-wee and the crew convince Randy he is cool enough without cigarettes.

© John Duke Kisch / CBS

Maybe I'm just twisted, but there's something kind of funny about seeing Randy smoking a cigarette. I wonder where the smoke would go in his little wooden body and exactly what the health risks would be. Regardless, what is most beneficial to kids and parents about Randy's experimentation with cigarettes is that the problem is corrected through positive peer-pressure. Pee-wee and his friends don't lecture Randy about the dangers of tobacco use, but instead appeal to his ego by telling him that he is cool and acceptable without it. This not only teaches the viewing audience to steer clear of cigarettes, but also to be nice to bullies like Randy, even if they aren't always nice to you in return.

The Secret Word of the Day: What
The King's Cartoon: *Flip the Frog: Puddle Pranks* (produced by Ub Iwerks in 1931)
Blink and You'll Miss: A claymation Pee-wee and some of the mutant toys make a cameo in the Penny cartoon.

1.09 • MONSTER IN THE PLAYHOUSE

Written by: George McGrath, John Paragon, Paul Reubens, Max Robert, and Michael Varhol
Directed by: Stephen R. Johnson
Original airdate: November 8, 1986

PEE-WEE DOUBTS the reports that a monster has broken loose in Puppetland until the giant, green, jibberish-growling cyclops makes his way to the playhouse. Although scared, Pee-wee asks Jambi for the ability to understand what the monster is saying. Jambi grants Pee-wee's wish and, within moments, Pee-wee learns that the monster, Roger, is just looking to make friends and shouldn't be judged by the way he looks. Throughout the rest of the episode, Pee-wee treats Roger as a respected guest.

Although Roger only appears in two episodes, he is a fan favorite. Many Pee-wee enthusiasts have noted that Roger looks remarkably like Mike Wazowski of the Pixar film *Monsters, Inc.* The dramatic tone of the episode's first half is fun to watch and may actually seem scary to some of the younger viewers in the audience. Despite the suspense, the episode should go a long way to helping those tykes who are afraid of creatures under their beds.

© John Duke Kisch / CBS

The Secret Word of the Day: Look

The King's Cartoon: *Jack Frost* (produced by Ub Iwerks in 1934)

Fun Fact: This is the only episode in the show's run in which Pee-wee doesn't ride his scooter alone during the end credits.

You May Remember: The Penny cartoons featured in this episode and the preceding one were edited together and shown during the Broadway run of *The Pee-wee Herman Show*.

Bet You Didn't Know: This is the first episode where Pee-wee and Magic Screen don't play connect-the-dots.

Blink and You'll Miss: Watch Reba closely as she leaves the playhouse. When she's visible through Mr. Window, you can see a different color blue on the sky backdrop. It's a door to exit the playhouse set which Reba reaches for right before the camera cuts to the next shot.

1.10 • THE COWBOY AND THE COWNTESS

Written by: George McGrath, John Paragon, Paul Reubens, Max Robert, and Michael Varhol
Directed by: Stephen R. Johnson
Original airdate: November 15, 1986

IF YOU HAVE a friend who hasn't seen *Pee-wee's Play-house* and wants to know why people find it interesting, tell them to start with "The Cowboy and the Cowntess." The episode has Pee-wee and Magic Screen scatting with the Puppet Band, the dinosaur family reviewing slides from their family vacation during which they met Ronald Reagan, and even some suggestive humor ("big feet, big boots").

This episode has gone down in *Playhouse* infamy for the way it plays with gender norms. Miss Yvonne asks Cowboy Curtis on a date, causing him to laugh at the idea of a woman asking a man out. Soon after, the Cowntess coaches Curtis on how to treat a woman while on a date, with Pee-wee filling in for Miss Yvonne. As Pee-wee and Curtis get close to sharing a kiss, Pee-wee exclaims that he's had enough and doesn't want to play anymore.

© John Duke Kisch / CBS

The Secret Word of the Day: Good
The King's Cartoon: *Mary's Little Lamb* (produced by Ub Iwerks in 1935)
Fun Fact: Although Cowboy Curtis and Miss Yvonne are not romantically involved throughout the series' run, this episode serves as a nice companion piece to the revival of *The Pee-wee Herman Show*, where the two express their feelings for one another.
Bet You Didn't Know: While *Playhouse* is revered for its visuals, this episode's score, which incorporates Western music themes, is particularly great to listen to. This may be because the music for this episode was composed by Danny Elfman, the musical genius that scored Pee-wee's first two feature films.
Blink and You'll Miss: Ever wondered what the playhouse looks like from inside Magic Screen? Watch closely at the end of the connect-the-dots segment and you'll get a peek.

1.11 • STOLEN APPLES

Written by: George McGrath, John Paragon, Paul Reubens, Max Robert, and Michael Varhol
Directed by: Stephen R. Johnson
Original airdate: November 22, 1986

© John Duke Kisch / CBS

RANDY GETS MRS. STEVE angry by stealing her apples and hiding them under Pee-wee's bed. After much back-and-forth, Mrs. Steve gets an apology from the puppet, but after she leaves, Randy tells Pee-wee his fingers were crossed as he was saying sorry.

While it's fun watching the playhouse bad-boy square off against the neighborhood snoop, this episode feels flat. *Pee-wee's Playhouse* can hardly be considered plot-driven entertainment, but the substance of this episode is particularly thin, with its best moments frontloaded in the first half.

The Secret Word of the Day: There
The King's Cartoon: *Somewhere in Dreamland* (produced by Dave Fleisher in 1936)
Fun Fact: The connect-the-dots sequence shares a few similarities with the plot of Alfred Hitchcock's *The Birds*.
You May Remember: A version of the "Pee-wee Herman Had a Farm" song in this episode is also in *Big Top Pee-wee*.
Blink and You'll Miss: When Pee-wee tosses Globey a treat, it changes from beige to red mid-throw. Also, careful observers will see a cigarette in the mouth of one of the members of the dinosaur family. Additionally, watch closely as the secret words are said while Pee-wee and Captain Carl are near the playhouse door and you'll see Pterri pop his head through the window, surprising both Paul Reubens and Phil Hartman.

1.12 • THE GANG'S ALL HERE

Written by: George McGrath, John Paragon, Paul Reubens, Max Robert, and Michael Varhol
Directed by: Stephen R. Johnson
Original airdate: November 29, 1986

THE PLAYHOUSE GANG arrives with Rusty, an old man they've befriended. The Gang plays with Pee-wee and helps him after his head gets stuck in the dinosaur family's hole.

This is another charming episode in the first season due largely to the presence of Calvert DeForest as Rusty. The juxtaposition between Rusty's actions and his age remind me of Edith Massey's bizarre performance as Divine's egg-loving mother in John Waters' *Pink Flamingos*. His age is never addressed and his character acts just as young, if not younger, than his prepubescent counterparts. It's a surreal experience to watch, but one that must be seen to be believed. Another episode highlight is Natasha Lyonne as Opal bugging Pee-wee with a barrage of "why" questions as he makes grilled cheese during snack time.

The Secret Word of the Day: Okay
The King's Cartoon: *Smile, Darn Ya, Smile!* (produced by Rudolf Ising in 1931)
Fun Fact: Calvert DeForest worked with Paul Reubens previously on the unreleased short film *Pee-wee's Lemonade Stand*.
You May Remember: Pee-wee gives each member of the Playhouse Gang a secret name, their name with an "o" sound following it, which is also borrowed material from his standup routine.
Blink and You'll Miss: Despite his youthful demeanor, Rusty's hat has a Playboy bunny pin stuck in it.

1.13 • PARTY

Written by: George McGrath, John Paragon, Paul Reubens, Max Robert, and Michael Varhol
Directed by: Stephen R. Johnson
Original airdate: December 6, 1986

PEE-WEE INVITES HIS friends over for a party. They play "Pin the Tail on the Conky" and spend lots of time dancing. Everyone has a good time celebrating their friendship and partying without due cause.

Although the set-up is simple, it's nice to see all the *Playhouse* characters under the same roof. This episode is the last of the first season and marks the final appearances of Mrs. Steve, Captain Carl, Dixie, and the original Playhouse Gang. For this reason alone, this episode is worth viewing — at least so you have a chance to say goodbye.

The Secret Word of the Day: This
The King's Cartoon: *Bunny Mooning* (produced by Dave Fleisher in 1937)
Fun Fact: Captain Carl and Miss Yvonne arrive together to the party, a reference to their relationship in the original *The Pee-wee Herman Show*.
You May Remember: The fridge in the dance pays homage to Pee-wee's big shoe dance in *Pee-wee's Big Adventure* by dancing to The Champs' song "Tequila." Later, Pee-wee calls himself "the luckiest boy in the world," a reference to *The Pee-wee Herman Show*.

SEASON 2

1987–1988

© Ken Sax

2.01 • OPEN HOUSE

Written by: George McGrath, Paul Reubens, and Max Robert
Directed by: Guy Louthan and Paul Reubens
Original airdate: September 12, 1987

MISS YVONNE SUGGESTS that Pee-wee have an open house so his friends can help him redecorate the playhouse. Ricardo and Cowboy Curtis are invited over and Pee-wee spends the majority of the day tricking them into cleaning for him. Along the way, Floory is discovered, Clocky arrives in the mail, and Mrs. Rene, the newest resident of Puppetland, appears for the first time.

"Open House" is an excellent moment in the series' run. The episode is the longest in the series, thanks to a truncated opening credits sequence, and it puts a creative spin on the logistic problem of the production changing shooting locations between the first two seasons. The entire set and the majority of the puppets received an upgrade, but with the playhouse in

© Ken Sax

disarray, the changes become acceptable, and even expected, for the viewing audience.

The Secret Word of the Day: House
The King's Cartoon: *The Little Broadcast* (produced by George Pal in 1943)
Fun Fact: Although "playhouse" is not exactly the secret word, the characters scream just as many times in this episode for that word as they do for "house." Additionally, this episode is the only to not have the full theme song.
Bet You Didn't Know: "Open House" is the first episode to show Pee-wee in clothing other than his signature gray suit.
Blink and You'll Miss: The Image Entertainment DVD release of this episode begins with a warning about the dangers of making sun tea, which Pee-wee is shown doing in one scene. According to the Center for Disease Control, warming tea with the sun can facilitate the growth of bacteria that can be hazardous if consumed. Because of the health risks, this scene was cut from the 1996 MGM/UA VHS releases and 1988–1989 Fox Family airings.

2.02 • PUPPY IN THE PLAYHOUSE

Written by: George McGrath, Paul Reubens, and Max Robert
Directed by: Wayne Orr and Paul Reubens
Original airdate: September 19, 1987

© Ken Sax

THE KING OF CARTOONS finds a puppy outside Pee-wee's playhouse, which Pee-wee decides to look after until he can find its owner. Throughout the day, the puppy wins over the hearts of Pee-wee and his friends, with the temporary exception of Pterri, who becomes jealous that the puppy is monopolizing Pee-wee's attention. When Reba comes by to deliver the mail, it's discovered that the lost puppy is hers, and Pee-wee promptly returns it.

As with the previous episode, "Puppy in the Playhouse" demonstrates how the writing in the series dramatically improved from one season to the next. While the first season had a number of memorable moments, the plot was usually secondary to random bits of fun and chaos. This episode sustains a straightforward plot while incorporating all of the silly elements associated with the series.

The Secret Word of the Day: Over
The King's Cartoon: *To Spring* (produced by Bill Hanna in 1936)
Blink and You'll Miss: Pay careful attention and you'll see the dinosaur family play with a Pee-wee Herman doll. Additionally, there is a visual reference to the California Raisins when food is taken from the fridge.
Bet You Didn't Know: According to George McGrath, Reubens hoped the playhouse puppy would become a recurring character in this show after this episode. However, Reubens became uncomfortable with the way the dog was treated by its trainer and held off introducing a regular playhouse animal until the show's fourth season.

© Ken Sax

2.03 • STORE

Written by: George McGrath, Paul Reubens, and Max Robert
Directed by: Wayne Orr and Paul Reubens
Original airdate: September 26, 1987

AFTER PEE-WEE, COWBOY CURTIS, and Reba all play inside Magic Screen, Miss Yvonne comes over. She, along with Pee-wee and Cowboy Curtis, decide to pretend the playhouse is Herman's Department Store, with Pee-wee playing the part of a salesman. The game continues until snack time.

The beginning sequences with Magic Screen are hilarious, especially with S. Epatha Merkerson's performance as the mail carrier who refuses to believe that two adults were just inside a tiny puppet. I always loved the way she seems both intrigued and confused by Pee-wee's behavior. Additionally, Cowboy Curtis's song "More" makes the episode worth a watch.

The Secret Word of the Day: More
The King's Cartoon: *Make 'Em Move* (produced by Harry Bailey and John Foster in 1931)
Fun Fact: When MGM/UA aired commercials to promote its 1996 VHS release of the series, a significant number of clips came from the department store sequence in this episode.
Bet You Didn't Know: This episode marks the first time people other than Pee-wee enter the Magic Screen.
Blink and You'll Miss: Watch carefully and you'll notice the frozen fruit cubes keep changing flavors over the course of the episode. Also, while Pee-wee is reading his pen pal letter, there is a quick reference to Australian pop singer Olivia Newton-John.

2.04 • PEE-WEE CATCHES A COLD

Written by: George McGrath, Paul Reubens, and Max Robert
Directed by: Wayne Orr and Paul Reubens
Original airdate: October 3, 1987

WHEN RICARDO DISCOVERS that Pee-wee is coming down with a cold, he encourages his friend to take it easy. Pee-wee ignores this advice and spends a lot of time playing. After several activities, he starts to feel worse and heads to bed. Miss Yvonne, dressed as a nurse, and Ricardo come back over to the playhouse at night to check-up on their friend, but Pee-wee is grumpy and snaps at them. Pee-wee falls back asleep after they leave and wakes up the next morning feeling better.

It's easy to empathize with Pee-wee in this episode. Staying in bed when you're sick is no fun, especially when there are so many cool toys for you to play with. However, the children in the viewing audience learn a valuable lesson about taking care of their bodies and health. The end sequence, with the food in the fridge talking about the four major food groups, is excellently animated and particularly educational.

The Secret Word of the Day: Out
The King's Cartoon: *The Sunshine Makers* (produced by Ed Eshbauch in 1935)
You May Remember: This is the episode with the famous "giant underpants" sequence. Pee-wee's giant underpants had previously been a staple of his standup comedy routine and the original *Pee-wee Herman Show.*
Blink and You'll Miss: When the characters are all sleeping, Globey's eyes are still open because the puppet was incapable of closing them.

2.05 • WHY WASN'T I INVITED?

Written by: George McGrath, Paul Reubens, and Max Robert
Directed by: Wayne Orr and Paul Reubens
Original airdate: October 10, 1987

PEE-WEE ISN'T INVITED to Cowntess's birthday party, causing him to wonder why he's been snubbed. He attempts to cheer himself up by playing and having a snack, but they're a waste of his time. After seeking the advice of a specialist, Pee-wee calls Cowntess on the picture phone to tell her that he feels hurt and doesn't want to be friends anymore. Moments later, Reba arrives with his invitation in the mail. Pee-wee apologizes to Cowntess and goes to the party.

Like "Open House," this episode cleverly creates a plot around production limitations. Because it would be extremely difficult for a puppet like Chairry to leave the playhouse, she is also uninvited to the Cowntess's party, whereas smaller puppets like Pterri and Globey would have little difficulty getting out through the playhouse door.

The Secret Word of the Day: All
The King's Cartoon: *Piano Tooners* (produced by John Foster and George Rufle in 1932)
Fun Fact: This is the only episode in which Chairry walks.
Blink and You'll Miss: When Magic Screen is trying to cheer up Pee-wee after he finds out he's not invited to the party, her mouth malfunctions.

© Ken Sax

2.06 • TONS OF FUN

Written by: George McGrath, Paul Reubens, and Max Robert
Directed by: Wayne Orr and Paul Reubens
Original airdate: October 17, 1987

THE PLAYHOUSE GANG comes over to play. After they leave, Cowboy Curtis comes by the playhouse to discover Pee-wee has left. Soon afterward Miss Yvonne arrives, does a clog dance, and makes ice cream pudding with Curtis as a surprise for Pee-wee.

Although the episode does have some funny moments, particularly the shots of Miss Yvonne in the bathtub, the writing is subpar. Pee-wee is absent for the majority of the episode and it's obvious that the playhouse is a little boring without him.

The Secret Word of the Day: Cool
The King's Cartoon: *The Little Broadcast* (produced by George Pal in 1943)
Fun Fact: The song Pee-wee and the puppets lip-synch to is "That Certain Feeling" by George and Ira Gershwin.
You May Remember: Miss Yvonne's peach cocktail dress was previously worn in "Store." The frock shows up in various other episodes in the series.

© Ken Sax

2.07 • SCHOOL

Written by: George McGrath, Paul Reubens, and Max Robert
Directed by: Wayne Orr and Paul Reubens
Original airdate: October 24, 1987

PEE-WEE PLAYS SCHOOL with the Playhouse Gang and teaches them about the discovery of America and the signing of the Declaration of Independence with the assistance of the Magic Screen's visuals and some stellar animation.

While the premise of this episode is simple, the Magic Screen animation, created by Dave Daniels, is worth the price of admission alone. Using a method called strata-cut, Daniels makes learning about history fun and unusually stunning for children and adults alike. The writers enhance those sequences even more by injecting a claymation Pee-wee into these historical events.

© Ken Sax

The Secret Word of the Day: Easy
The King's Cartoon: *Neptune Nonsense* (produced by Burt Gillett in 1936)
Fun Fact: Lil' Punkin (Alisan Porter) sings "Broadway Baby" by Stephen Sondheim, about a person determined to make it on Broadway. Coincidentally, Alisan did make it to the Great White Way when she starred in the 2006 revival of *A Chorus Line*. Additionally, this episode makes Rapunzel the first person besides Pee-wee to get the secret word from Conky.
You May Remember: The dinosaur family makes a dancing Pee-wee Herman figure out of pipe cleaners. As it dances, "Tequila" plays in the background, just as in *Pee-wee's Big Adventure* and the earlier "Party" episode of *Playhouse*. Also, Pee-wee's pledge of allegiance is similar to the one at the beginning of the revival of *The Pee-wee Herman Show*.

2.08 • SPRING

Written by: George McGrath, Paul Reubens, and Max Robert
Directed by: Wayne Orr and Paul Reubens
Original airdate: October 31, 1987

COWBOY CURTIS COMES by the playhouse and shows Pee-wee how to grow a plant in a glass. Soon after, the King of Cartoons arrives along with his wife and new son. Later, Pee-wee tries out for the little league team, but doesn't make it. Ricardo reminds him there are lots of sports in the world and encourages Pee-wee to find the one that's just right for his talents.

"Spring" is another episode with a simple, yet well-executed, concept. There isn't really too much going on, but the parts all add up nicely. The King of Cartoons is given a little character development in this episode and, as one would expect, the educational video about where babies come from is both appropriately vague and comprehensible to children.

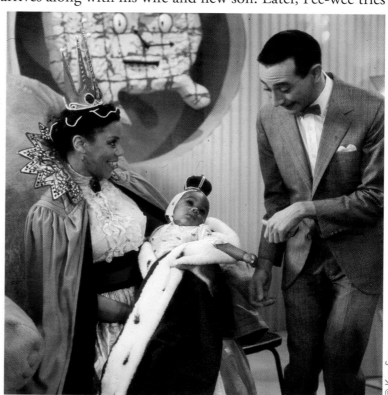

© Ken Sax

The Secret Word of the Day: Begin
The King's Cartoon: *Much Ado about Mutton* (produced by Isador Sparber in 1947)
Fun Fact: Randy makes a quick reference to Howdy Doody, the classic marionette who was the inspiration for Randy's looks.

2.09 • PLAYHOUSE IN OUTER SPACE

Written by: George McGrath, Paul Reubens, and Max Robert
Directed by: Wayne Orr and Paul Reubens
Original airdate: November 7, 1987

© Ken Sax

THE PLAYHOUSE, ALONG with Reba the Mail Lady, is blasted into outer space. Once it lands, a female alien named Miss Yvona, who bears a striking resemblance to Miss Yvonne, attempts to warn Pee-wee about Zyzzybalubah, the alien with a bad personality who is solely responsible for them being there. Soon Zyzzybalubah comes in, puts an invisible force field in the playhouse, and forces everyone to play with him. Pee-wee tells him that one shouldn't try to get friends by force, and Zyzzybalubah apologizes. The playhouse characters teach him how to make friends properly and they return with him to Earth to play.

This was one of my favorite *Playhouse* episodes when I was a kid. Not only do we get to see Pee-wee's pals in another setting beyond Puppetland, we get to meet new out-of-this-world characters. From an educational standpoint, this episode teaches a great deal about the planets and our solar system in a way that is engaging and might almost be received subconsciously by children. Finally, the opportunity to hear Reba and Pee-wee harmonize on "The Whistle Song" is the cherry on top of the sundae.

The Secret Word of the Day: Zyzzybalubah

The King's Cartoon: *Ship of the Ether* (produced by George Pal in 1934)

Fun Fact: Cowboy Curtis's horse is named Pegasus in this episode, but in the revival of *The Pee-wee Herman Show* he rides a mare named Ginger.

Blink and You'll Miss: Although Pluto is no longer classified as a planet, it appears in this episode during Pee-wee's ride through space.

© Ken Sax

2.10 • PAJAMA PARTY

Written by: George McGrath, Paul Reubens, and Max Robert
Directed by: Wayne Orr and Paul Reubens
Original airdate: November 14, 1987

© Ken Sax

PEE-WEE HAS A pajama party with all of his pals. They spend time playing party games, reading bedtime stories, and making shadow puppets. At the end of the episode, Pee-wee makes a bowl of fruit salad as a midnight snack and, because he loves it so much, gets married to it.

Much has been written about the ending sequence of this episode, where Pee-wee marries the bowl of fruit salad. Is it a dismissal of the sanctity of marriage? Is it a glimpse into the character's sexual preferences? According to cowriter George McGrath, it's just good, silly fun: "I am almost positive that if the thought that the fruit salad marriage would be interpreted as some sort of homosexuality reference, Paul would have made sure it was changed. I don't think anything in the series was ever meant to imply homosexuality, or cater to the gay community, at least in the episodes I was involved with writing. It just happened that a lot of our humor did that just because of . . . well . . . you figure it out!" Regardless of the reasons why this scene was included, the fruit salad marriage marks a moment that many people remember well from the series and cite as an example of the show's irreverent humor — a mix of cheeky and innocent that plays well for children and adults.

The Secret Word of the Day: Watch

The King's Cartoon: *Musical Memories* (produced by Dave Fleischer in 1935)

Fun Fact: The guy that calls the playhouse accidentally is art director and puppeteer Wayne White in his only on-screen cameo.

You May Remember: During the puppet dance, Pee-wee does his big-shoe dance from his standup routine and from *Pee-wee's Big Adventure*. Pee-wee's reading of Jane Thayer's *Part-Time Dog* was repeated in the revival of *The Pee-wee Herman Show*.

© Ken Sax

SEASON 3

1988–1989

© Ken Sax

3.01 • REBA EATS AND PTERRI RUNS
Written by: John Paragon
Directed by: Wayne Orr and Paul Reubens
Original airdate: September 10, 1988

PEE-WEE USES JAMBI to transport Reba to the playhouse so she can mail a pen pal letter for him. After his wish is granted, Reba magically appears and immediately expresses her frustration about being inconvenienced on her day off. Pee-wee makes it up to her by preparing an imaginary breakfast. Throughout the episode, Pee-wee yells at Pterri so Randy encourages him to run away. The playhouse inhabitants launch a search for the fugitive pterodactyl and are relieved to find that he was just hiding because he thought no one liked him. Pee-wee reminds Pterri, and the viewing audience, that running away from your problems is never the answer.

This episode is a must-watch for parents with small children. The first half is genuinely entertaining, especially with Reba's wild reactions to the imaginary breakfast. The second half, however, offers an important lesson for children. There may be days when your parents might seem like they don't like you, but they still love you.

The Secret Word of the Day: Now
The King's Cartoon: *Farm Foolery* (produced by Seymour Kneitel in 1949)
Bet You Didn't Know: The Image Entertainment DVD release of this episode omits the "My Name Is" song that begins this episode. This song was present in the 1996 VHS release. The reason for the omission is unknown.
Blink and You'll Miss: During the imaginary breakfast, Pee-wee refers to the puppets as "characters," a bizarre phraseology if we're supposed to believe they are all actual and alive.

3.02 • TO TELL THE TOOTH

Written by: John Paragon
Directed by: Wayne Orr and Paul Reubens
Original airdate: September 17, 1988

© Ken Sax

PEE-WEE HAS A toothache, but is afraid to go to the dentist. After trying one of Randy's dangerous home remedies, Pee-wee listens to the advice of Miss Yvonne and the puppets and he goes to see a dentist. He comes back without pain and with a wisdom tooth in hand.

This episode gets a lot of mileage out of a simple premise. From the opening sequence with Randy's bad breath, to Pee-wee returning on a gurney after his dentist visit, there are a lot of laughs to be had in one short half hour. If you don't burst into a fit of giggles watching the dummy dressed as Pee-wee getting dragged across the playhouse floor, you may be lacking a pulse.

The Secret Word of the Day: It
The King's Cartoon: *An Elephant Never Forgets* (produced by Dave Fleisher in 1935)
Bet You Didn't Know: *Pee-wee's Playhouse* won six Daytime Emmy Awards for this episode. Charles Randazzo, Peter W. Moyer, David Pincus, and Steve Purcell won for Outstanding Achievement in Videotape Editing, while Yolanda Toussieng and Jerry Masone won for Outstanding Achievement in Hairstyling.
Blink and You'll Miss: Jambi's head is superimposed over Abraham Lincoln's on Mt. Rushmore during the end credits.

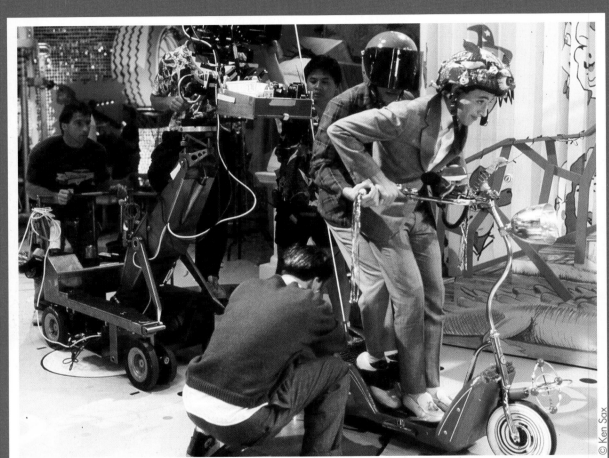

© Ken Sax

SEASON 4

1989–1990

4.01 • PEE-WEE AND THE DEL RUBIOS

Written by: John Paragon
Directed by: John Paragon and Paul Reubens
Original airdate: September 9, 1989

REBA HAS A splinter and uses the services of Dr. Pee-wee to have it removed. Later, the Del Rubio Triplets come by to sing a psychedelic rendition of Nancy Sinatra's "These Boots Were Made for Walking."

If "Open House" was an excellent way to start a new *Playhouse* season, this episode was a horrendous one. While the Del Rubio Triplets are certainly kitschy, they seem overwhelmingly out of place in the playhouse. Worse, the break in the middle of the episode, where the trio sings, is awkward and uninteresting to watch.

The Secret Word of the Day: Well
The King's Cartoon: *Hunky & Spunky* (produced by Dave Fleischer in 1938)
Fun Fact: This episode is the first to include Chandelier, Roosevelt, and an El Hombre cartoon.
Bet You Didn't Know: The Del Rubio Triplets were introduced to Paul Reubens by songwriter Allee Willis, who collaborated with Pee-wee Herman on the song "Big Adventure."
You May Remember: Pee-wee uses the mirror on his doctor headband to look up Reba's dress, much like he does to Susan in the original *The Pee-wee Herman Show*.

4.02 • FIRE IN THE PLAYHOUSE

Written by: John Paragon
Directed by: John Paragon and Paul Reubens
Original airdate: September 16, 1989

PEE-WEE DREAMS ABOUT being Super Pee-wee, saving Miss Yvonne trapped under a barbell. Just as she is about to give him a thank-you kiss, Pee-wee is woken up for snack time. Miss Yvonne bakes bread for their peanut butter and jelly sandwiches, but impatient Randy turns up the heat and causes the bread to burn. Fireman Frank comes by, puts out the fire, and teaches everyone about fire safety.

This episode is an excellent one for parents to watch with their kids, especially with the educational lesson. Parents would have the added treat of some suggestive humor that's likely to soar over the heads of most children. Watching Miss Yvonne flirt with Fireman Frank is fun, especially since he is so deadpan and seemingly disinterested in her romantic advances.

© Ken Sax

The Secret Word of the Day: One
The King's Cartoon: *The Stork Market* (produced by Seymour Kneitel in 1949)
Bet You Didn't Know: In the event that CBS's standards and practices department would veto the joke about Miss Yvonne having a smoke detector over her bed, Lynne Stewart recorded a near-identical scene in which she says she has a "smoke detector in [her] kitchen over the sink."
You May Remember: When Pee-wee makes fun of Miss Yvonne's flirting with Fireman Frank, it's similar to the way he made fun of her relationship with Kap'n Karl in the original *Pee-wee Herman Show*.
Blink and You'll Miss: When Miss Yvonne gets trapped under the dumbbell, the bar is bent around her bust.

4.03 • LOVE THAT STORY

Written by: Max Robert
Directed by: John Paragon and Paul Reubens
Original airdate: September 23, 1989

PEE-WEE AND MISS YVONNE decide to play library with the puppets, and Pee-wee turns into a tyrannical librarian. Afterwards, Ricardo comes over to show off his new ballet moves and Miss Yvonne dances the hula.

"Love That Story" is an interesting concept for an episode. It's important for children to learn that a story can be told in many different ways and Pee-wee and his pals teach that lesson in a creative way. It would have been nice to have included Miss Yvonne's interpretative dance from earlier in the series as an additional method of creative storytelling.

The Secret Word of the Day: End
The King's Cartoon: *Spring Song* (produced by Isador Sparber in 1949)
You May Remember: The book Miss Yvonne wants to check out from the library is the fictitious *Part-Time Dog: Part Two*, a reference to the book Pee-wee read in last season's "Pajama Party." Additionally, Pee-wee does his big-shoe dance during the Nutcracker performance with Ricardo.
Blink and You'll Miss: This is the first episode in which the classic cartoon is not introduced by the King.

© Ken Sax

4.04 • SICK, DID SOMEBODY SAY SICK?

Written by: John Paragon
Directed by: John Paragon and Paul Reubens
Original airdate: September 30, 1989

© John Duke Kisch / CBS

PEE-WEE MAKES A wish to go to Paris, but Jambi is unable to grant it because he's sick. After calling a genie-ologist, Pee-wee learns that Jambi is suffering from a disease called "mekka lekka hi mekka hineyitis." To cure the disease, Dr. Jinga-Janga suggests that Pee-wee remind Jambi how much he is appreciated around the playhouse. Pee-wee does, and Jambi feels better.

It's nice to have an episode centered on Jambi, a favorite character for many fans. However, because he is sick, there isn't a ton for the character to do in this episode. The opening moments of the episode set in "Randy's Playhouse" are clever, as is the animated sequence of Jambi's head adjusting to his sickness. The animation on that particular segment was done by Dave Daniels.

The Secret Word of the Day: Go
The King's Cartoon: *To Spring* (produced by Hugh Harman and Rudolf Isling in 1936)
Fun Fact: In this episode, Randy gets the secret word from Conky while Pee-wee is out of the playhouse. Being the mischief-maker he is, Randy makes everyone bark like a dog instead of scream after hearing the secret word.
Bet You Didn't Know: Dr. Jinga-Janga, the "wish doctor" played by Bernard Fox, is a reference to Dr. Bombay, the "witch doctor" on *Bewitched*.

© Ken Sax

4.05 • MISS YVONNE'S VISIT

Written by: Doug Cox and John Moody
Directed by: John Paragon and Paul Reubens
Original airdate: October 7, 1989

MISS YVONNE IS GETTING her house painted and asks Pee-wee if she can stay over for a few days. At first he's excited about having company, but it doesn't take long for her to overstay her welcome. By cluttering up the playhouse and spending hours on the picture phone, she slowly makes Pee-wee regret inviting her in the first place. With the help of Jambi, Pee-wee accelerates the painting of her house, allowing Miss Yvonne to make a quick return home.

Most everyone has experienced a house-guest who overstays his or her welcome, and "Miss Yvonne's Visit" perfectly illustrates how one can be torn between wanting to spend time with a good friend and wanting privacy and normality to return. Kudos to writers Doug Cox and John Moody, who are careful not to vilify Miss Yvonne by portraying her as a completely narcissistic monster. When she makes Pee-wee breakfast and genuinely expresses her gratitude for his hospitality, the audience is reminded why the two are such good friends.

The Secret Word of the Day: Nice
Fun Fact: Pee-wee's picture phone backdrop has him filling in for the farmer in Grant Wood's *American Gothic* painting. Additionally, this is the first episode to not include a classic cartoon.
Bet You Didn't Know: The writers had originally planned for a sequence where Miss Yvonne's wigs would be hanging from a clothing line in the playhouse, but Paul Reubens nixed the joke, worried that it would ruin the illusion of her hair being real.
Blink and You'll Miss: The painter responsible for sprucing up Miss Yvonne's ceiling is named Michael Angelo, a reference to artist Michaelangelo and the ceiling of the Sistine Chapel.

4.06 • REBARELLA

Written by: Lynne Stewart and Mimi Pond
Directed by: John Paragon and Paul Reubens
Original airdate: October 14, 1989

Courtesy CBS / PhotoFest © CBS

PEE-WEE AND HIS friends pretend they are flying in an airplane, but their playtime is interrupted when Reba comes over to talk about a problem. She has a big crush on a fireman named Derrick, who recently asked her out on a date, but she's nervous and doesn't know how to act. Miss Yvonne gives her a beauty makeover, which transforms Reba's self-esteem.

Pee-wee suggests that Reba and Derrick have their date in the playhouse, using the Magic Screen to help recreate a drive-in movie setting. The two hit it off and end the night with a kiss.

"Rebarella" is an amazingly entertaining episode that revisits themes from both "The Cowboy and the Cowntess" and "Beauty Makeover" from the first season. The episode marks the *Playhouse* writing debut for Lynne Stewart and for Mimi Pond, Wayne White's wife. Although this is Reba's last appearance in the series, with the exception of clips from previous episodes, she is given an excellent send-off with a touching and funny episode centered on her character.

The Secret Word of the Day: Stop
The King's Cartoon: *The Kids in the Shoe* (produced by Dave Fleisher in 1935)
Fun Fact: When Globey says "the plane, the plane," it's an allusion to Hervé Villechaize's character on the hit television show *Fantasy Island*. Also, this is the only episode where the credits don't scroll over footage of Pee-wee riding his scooter.
You May Remember: As a part of her beauty makeover, Reba wears a bouffant wig similar to Miss Yvonne's and even borrows one of the most beautiful woman in Puppetland's favorite dresses.
Blink and You'll Miss: The imaginary plane ride takes place on "flight eleven-teen." Additionally, Billy Baloney magically moves by himself during the plane sequences, despite Pee-wee being in the front of the plane. Finally, Conky asks to read a *Playrobot* magazine on the flight, a reference for grown-ups to both *Playboy* and *Playgirl* adult magazines.

4.07 • HEAT WAVE

Written by: Rob Bragin
Directed by: John Paragon and Paul Reubens
Original airdate: October 21, 1989

IT'S UNBEARABLY HOT in Puppetland, causing the flowers to wilt. The temperature rises even more when Miss Yvonne and Mrs. Rene come to the playhouse to show off the same one-of-a-kind dress designed by a French designer. Pee-wee has a trial to decide which woman should be allowed to wear the dress. When the ladies' bickering turns to attempted bribery of the Honorable Pee-wee Herman, the designer himself is brought in to settle the score.

© Ken Sax

"Heat Wave" is a curiously titled episode, especially since much of it takes place during the sober courtroom sequence. Watching Miss Yvonne and Mrs. Rene go at it over fashion is fun, along with the chance to see Pee-wee rule with an iron fist, much like he did in the earlier "Love That Story" episode.

The Secret Words of the Day: Hear and Here
The King's Cartoon: *The Song of the Birds* (produced by Dave Fleisher in 1935)
Fun Fact: Elvis makes his second appearance in consecutive Penny cartoons. The King had a brief cameo in last episode's "Rebarella." This is also the only episode with two secret words.

4.08 • CHAIRRY-TEE DRIVE

Written by: John Paragon
Directed by: Wayne Orr and Paul Reubens
Original airdate: October 28, 1989

PEE-WEE SEARCHES THE playhouse frantically for the Cowntess's pencil sharpener, which she let him borrow and he has not yet returned. While rummaging through his clutter, he decides to donate a lot of old items to charity. The rest of the residents of Puppetland chip in, occasionally having fun with the items found along the way.

Despite a relatively weak premise, this episode succeeds due to some very funny moments. The Cowntess repeatedly asking for her pencil sharpener causes laughter, despite the predictable ending when she realizes she's had it at her barn all along. And the flashback to a young Pee-wee Herman playing with Baby Pterri is a nice touch.

The Secret Word of the Day: Wait
Fun Fact: Pee-wee dances in high-heel shoes to Peggy Lee's "Fever."
Bet You Didn't Know: The educational video about traffic is narrated by James Stewart.

© Ken Sax

4.09 • LET'S PLAY OFFICE

Written by: John Paragon and Lynne Stewart
Directed by: Wayne Orr and Paul Reubens
Original airdate: November 4, 1989

© Ken Sax

PEE-WEE AND MISS YVONNE decide to play office. Pee-wee acts as the boss, while Miss Yvonne is stuck being the secretary. In typical fashion, he becomes a bully and makes her job difficult. When the two switch positions, Pee-wee takes an extended break by the water cooler.

"Let's Play Office" is similar in tone to several earlier episodes this season, but for some reason, it falls flat. The play between Pee-wee and Miss Yvonne is similar to "Love That Story" and "Rebarella," and the friendship between Miss Yvonne and Cowntess comes back to life. But, despite some funny moments, "Let's Play Office" is constructed around one gag and some sewn-together elements from previous installments.

The Secret Word of the Day: That
The King's Cartoon: *Little Lambkins* (produced by Dave Fleisher in 1940)
Fun Fact: This is the only time Jambi appears outside his box.

4.10 • I REMEMBER CURTIS

Written by: John Paragon
Directed by: John Paragon and Paul Reubens
Original airdate: November 11, 1989

© Ken Sax

WHEN PEE-WEE REALIZES Cowboy Curtis forgot his magic lasso at the playhouse, he invites the cowboy over to play and retrieve his rope. This leads to a series of reminiscences from the *Playhouse* characters about fun times they have had with Cowboy Curtis.

Flashback episodes are typically weak, and this episode doesn't even have the benefit of a strong premise. It's fitting that a season that began with the awkward Del Rubio Triplets be concluded with an episode with less than 10 minutes of original material in it. While most of the clips are of stories worth revisiting, it's better to watch the original episodes than to waste your time with this.

The Secret Word of the Day: Remember

Fun Fact: When Pee-wee says, "Tune in next week, same Pee-wee time, same Pee-wee channel," he's making a reference to the 1960s television show *Batman*.

You May Remember: This episode includes clips from "Store," "Rainy Day," "Pajama Party," and "The Cowboy and the Cowntess."

Blink and You'll Miss: When Pee-wee tries to get Cowboy Curtis's boots, there's a quick visual reference to the Wicked Witch of the West in *The Wizard of Oz* (sparks fly off Curtis's boots in much the same way Dorothy's shoes send out sparks to prevent the witch from taking them).

© Ken Sax

SEASON 5

1990–1991

5.01 • CONKY'S BREAKDOWN

Written by: John Moody and Doug Cox
Directed by: John Paragon and Paul Reubens
Original airdate: September 9, 1990

© Ken Sax

CONKY HAS DIFFICULTY printing the secret word, and soon after, he tells Pee-wee he's feeling sick. Pee-wee attempts to fix Conky himself, but can't make heads or tails of the meticulous directions in the instruction manual. He decides to call his authorized Conky repairman who has the robot fixed in no time.

This episode is one of the most famous of the show's final season. One can almost imagine the children watching at home becoming sad as their favorite robot falls sick, then excited when he is put back together. Jimmy Smits' cameo as the repairman is classic, along with Miss Yvonne's heavy-handed flirting. It's not every day you can ask "Is that a wrench in your pocket?" on children's television and get away with it!

The Secret Word of the Day: Great
The King's Cartoon: *One More Time* (produced by Rudolf Ising in 1931)
Fun Fact: The secret word initially comes out as "Grrrrr" due to Conky's malfunction.
You May Remember: Pee-wee fawns over a centerfold of a Schwinn, a reference to his beloved bicycle in *Pee-wee's Big Adventure*.

5.02 • MYSTERY

Written by: David Cohen and S.H. Schulman
Directed by: John Paragon and Paul Reubens
Original airdate: September 15, 1990

PEE-WEE CAN'T FIND one of his suits, a bowl, a spoon, his photo album, and his dots for playing inside the Magic Screen. He holds his friends on trial for the theft, but absolves them of guilt after he catches a man named Busby sneaking out of the playhouse with his belongings. Busby tells Pee-wee he stole the things because he was new to the neighborhood and, seeing as Pee-wee had a lot of friends, thought he could attract people if he tried to become more like Pee-wee. Pee-wee decides to let Busby off the hook and befriend him instead of calling the police.

Although this episode has a lot of filler, like a lengthy classic cartoon, it's surprisingly engaging. The final sequence with Busby is both hilarious and frightening at the same time, along with the recurring joke of the organist playing a chord after Pee-wee screams, "It's a mystery!" While not one of the strongest installments in the series, "Mystery" is certainly a highlight of the tepid fifth season.

The Secret Word of the Day: Around
The King's Cartoon: *Farm Frolics* (produced by Bob Clampett in 1941)
Fun Fact: This is the first episode where the secret word is screamed after it is read.
Bet You Didn't Know: The creepy organist is Max Robert, cowriter on all episodes for the first two seasons.
You May Remember: The food in the refrigerator watches a brief scene from *Big Top Pee-wee.*

5.03 • FRONT PAGE PEE-WEE

Written by: John Moody and Doug Cox
Directed by: John Paragon and Paul Reubens
Original airdate: September 22, 1990

PEE-WEE AND HIS friends decide to print a newspaper about the fun things going on in the playhouse. Although everyone contributes articles and photographs, they are horrified to see the finished product — a paper full of lies and gossip. It turns out Randy edited the paper after Pee-wee went to sleep in an attempt to "spice it up." Pee-wee tells Randy that making up lies is never good, especially in print.

"Front Page Pee-wee" suffers the same malady as do many episodes in the fifth season. The writers seem either fatigued with or disinterested in the show. The premise seems promising enough, but there really aren't any memorable or funny moments in this episode to make it worth watching.

The Secret Word of the Day: How
The King's Cartoon: *The Little Red Hen* (produced by Ub Iwerks in 1934)
Fun Fact: The educational video about making ice cream is voiced by John Paragon.

© Ken Sax

5.04 • TANGO TIME
Written by: David Cohen and S.H. Schulman
Directed by: John Paragon and Paul Reubens
Original airdate: September 29, 1990

AFTER SPENDING A day playing, Pee-wee helps Mrs. Rene learn how to tango using his magic footprints. Ultimately, Pee-wee sweeps her off her feet, literally, and then reminisces about the good old days with Cowboy Curtis and the puppets.

When critics offer evidence that *Pee-wee's Playhouse* "jumped the shark," this is the episode they refer to. The show's half hour is stuffed with filler material, beginning with Roosevelt eating a can of dog food for nearly two minutes, the King showing two lengthy cartoons, and faux flashbacks at the end. There is barely a plot to speak of in this episode and what is there isn't very strong.

The Secret Word of the Day: Fast
The King's Cartoons: *Freddy the Freshman* (produced by Rudolf Ising in 1932) and *Humpty Dumpty* (produced by Ub Iwerks in 1935)
Fun Fact: This is the first episode to include two classic cartoons. Also, this is the only episode to show the characters outside on the playhouse deck.
Bet You Didn't Know: There's a reason the King of Cartoons sounds so comfortable reciting Hamlet's classic "To be or not to be" speech. Before hosting cartoons at the playhouse, William Marshall was a Shakespearean actor who had starred in many productions in North America and Europe.

5.05 • PLAYHOUSE DAY

Written by: Rob Bragin
Directed by: John Paragon and Paul Reubens
Original airdate: October 6, 1990

PEE-WEE BECOMES BUMMED out when Cowboy Curtis and Miss Yvonne can't come over and play because they have to work. Pee-wee and the puppets decide to pretend it is a holiday so they could have fun together. When the King of Cartoons declares Playhouse Day an official holiday, Cowboy Curtis and Miss Yvonne come right over to celebrate.

"Playhouse Day" has a paper-thin plot, but the anything-goes atmosphere makes for an episode one can sit through. The final sequence at the parade is just silly enough to make you giggle.

The Secret Word of the Day: Thing
The King's Cartoons: *Fin N' Catty* (produced by Chuck Jones in 1943)
Fun Fact: During the parade, the band plays "Louie Louie," made famous by The Kingsmen.
You May Remember: Pee-wee's big-shoe dance comes back in this episode during the parade sequence.
Blink and You'll Miss: While most of the *Playhouse* characters are easy to spot during the parade, keep your eyes open for Roosevelt and Mr. Kite.

© Ken Sax

5.06 • ACCIDENTAL PLAYHOUSE

Written by: John Moody and Doug Cox
Directed by: John Paragon and Paul Reubens
Original airdate: October 13, 1990

© Ken Sax

PEE-WEE RECEIVES A pen pal letter from his friend Oki Doki in Japan telling him that he's coming to visit. Within moments, Oki arrives at the playhouse. During Oki's visit, Pee-wee learns about Japanese culture.

"Accidental Playhouse" is a particularly fun episode, primarily because of all of the Japanese culture infused into the half hour. Globey's recap of his tour to Japan is entertaining to watch, along with Oki introducing Pee-wee to sushi and to dubbed, Godzilla-type films. Although Pee-wee occasionally seems disinterested, most people would certainly find something of value in this episode.

The Secret Word of the Day: Place
The King's Cartoon: *Sinkin' in the Bathtub* (produced by Hugh Harman and Rudolf Ising in 1930)
Fun Fact: This is the only episode where the secret word is said and flashed on the screen in a different language.

5.07 • FUN, FUN, FUN

Written by: Max Robert
Directed by: John Paragon and Paul Reubens
Original airdate: October 20, 1990

PEE-WEE WATCHES A "MOO-VIE" (get it?) produced by Cowntess and then has fun making cheese balls with Miss Yvonne. The rest of his day is spent making a mobile out of construction paper and coat hangers and getting fit by doing aerobics.

   As the title suggests, this is another episode devoid of a significant plot. The majority of the segments aren't well executed or interesting to watch. For example, when Pee-wee makes the mobile, he has difficulty cutting the string because of the safety scissors he's using. Then he occasionally has to maneuver the yarn to keep the construction paper figures from colliding with one another. The episode seems hastily put together from start to finish.

The Secret Word of the Day: On
The King's Cartoon: *Freddy the Freshman* (produced by Rudolf Isling in 1932)

© Ken Sax

5.08 • CAMPING OUT

Written by: John Paragon
Directed by: John Paragon and Paul Reubens
Original airdate: October 27, 1990

© Ken Sax

PEE-WEE AND COWBOY CURTIS go camping in the Grand Canyon. While there, they have a weenie roast and talk about the beauty of nature. While they are gone, Mrs. Rene playhouse-sits and keeps the puppets entertained.

"Camping Out" is really the last episode worth watching in this series. While it's unfortunate to leave so many *Playhouse* characters behind, it is a nice change of pace to see Pee-wee and Cowboy Curtis alone with the elements. Their conversations are poignant without being too sappy and they still manage to have fun cracking jokes and singing.

The Secret Word of the Day: Wait
The King's Cartoons: *Allegretto* (produced by Oskar Fischinger in 1936) and *Balloon Land* (produced by Ub Iwerks in 1935)
You May Remember: The footage inside the fridge is exactly the same as in "Mystery," except this time the food is watching *Sesame Street* instead of *Big Top Pee-wee*. And the *Balloon Land* cartoon was shown during the 1981 and Club Nokia runs of *The Pee-wee Herman Show*. It was replaced during the Broadway run with a Penny cartoon.

© Ken Sax

5.09 • SOMETHING TO DO

Written by: John Paragon
Directed by: John Paragon and Paul Reubens
Original airdate: November 3, 1990

PEE-WEE'S BORED, SO JAMBI gives him a list of things to do. Pee-wee begins by drawing a self-portrait, moves on to blowing up a balloon, and finishes up by taking a walk with Miss Yvonne past the flowers and the waterfall picture hanging up in the playhouse.

"Something to Do" is a better executed version of "Fun, Fun, Fun," but still suffers from a lack of purpose. The activities Pee-wee engages in during this episode are at least entertaining to watch. However, the episode loses points for the ill-placed musical interlude thrown in during the last few minutes.

The Secret Word of the Day: Do

Fun Fact: Pee-wee and Miss Yvonne lip-synch to "By a Waterfall" from the film *Footlight Parade.*

You May Remember: Pee-wee repeats his routine of letting the air out of a balloon in the revival of *The Pee-wee Herman Show*. And the "My Name Is" song from the third season's "Reba Eats and Pterri Runs" is back in this episode.

5.10 • PLAYHOUSE FOR SALE

Written by: John Paragon
Directed by: John Paragon and Paul Reubens
Original airdate: November 10, 1990

IN THIS FINAL episode of *Pee-wee's Playhouse*, Miss Yvonne comes by the playhouse to visit, but Pee-wee isn't there. Within a few moments, she discovers a "for sale" sign in the window. The characters all begin reminiscing about the good times they had and wondering what will become of them without a playhouse. When Pee-wee arrives, he explains that the sign originally was advertising lemonade for sale, but a portion of the sign fell off.

While there is a certain rationale behind ending a series with a clip show, it always feels boring and contrite. *Pee-wee's Playhouse* was one of the most innovative shows on television and to end the show's run with a barrage of flashbacks does a mild disservice to all the preceding episodes. It's also hard to sit through an episode of the show where Pee-wee is present for less than three minutes. "Playhouse for Sale" is an unfortunate ending to an extraordinary series.

The Secret Word of the Day: Word

Fun Fact: The song that plays over the montage is "The Way We Were," performed by Charlotte Crossley.

You May Remember: This episode includes clips from "Reba Eats and Pterri Runs," "Open House," "Chairry-Tee Drive," "Love That Story," "Spring," "Store," "Dr. Pee-wee and the Del Rubios," "Pee-wee Catches a Cold," "Tons of Fun," "Playhouse Day," "Miss Yvonne's Visit," "Rebarella," "Front Page Pee-wee," "Tango Time," "Sick? Did Somebody Say Sick?," "Fire in the Playhouse," "Pajama Party," and *Pee-wee's Playhouse Christmas Special*. Miss Yvonne performs her ballet with the same music and choreography as in the original *Pee-wee Herman Show*. Also Pee-wee says he wouldn't sell the playhouse, not even for "a million, billion, trillion, zillion dollars." This same amount was ruled out in *Pee-wee's Big Adventure* when Francis was trying to negotiate a price for Pee-wee's bicycle.

AFTERWORD

THE PEE-WEE HERMAN SHOW had its official opening on November 11, 2010, with a red carpet event attended by Alan Cumming, Rosie O'Donnell, Chita Rivera, Susan Sarandon, John Waters, Wendy Williams, and *Playhouse* alumni S. Epatha Merkerson and Natasha Lyonne, among others. The show received overwhelmingly positive reviews from nearly all major news outlets, with the *New York Times* declaring the show "yummier than chocolate!"

Pee-wee's Broadway run was an undeniable success, generating over $6.3 million in ticket sales alone in during its 10-week engagement. The show ran for 18 previews and 62 regular performances. The comeback of Pee-wee Herman placed second on the *New York Times*' list of 110 topics New Yorkers were discussing most in 2010.

On December 21, 2010, weeks before the show was scheduled to close on January 2, 2011, it was announced that HBO would air a special presentation of *The Pee-wee Herman Show* on March 19, 2011, that would be taped a couple of months earlier on January 6. Nancy Geller, senior vice president of HBO original programming, put it best in a press release: "Before his hit series and movies, HBO introduced Paul Reubens' Pee-wee Herman to a national audience in the 'Young Comedians' series, followed by the groundbreaking 1981 special. It's thrilling to have Paul back on the network, and it will be a blast to return to Pee-wee's playhouse."

Pee-wee's fans, whether they were first introduced to him in the 1980s or late 2000s, couldn't agree with her more.

THE PUPPETLAND DIRECTORY

Richard Abramson: Paul Reubens' manager (1984–1987), producer of *Pee-wee's Big Adventure*, and executive producer of *Pee-wee's Playhouse* (1986–1987) and *Big Top Pee-wee*.

Lori Alan: Understudy and vocal actress for the Los Angeles run of *The Pee-wee Herman Show* (2010).

Craig Bartlett: Animator on *Pee-wee's Playhouse* (1987–1991).

Steve Binder: Producer of *Pee-wee's Playhouse* (1987–1989) and *Pee-wee's Playhouse Christmas Special*.

Kent Burton: Animator for *Pee-wee's Playhouse* (1986–1987, 1989–1991).

Tim Burton: Director of *Pee-wee's Big Adventure*.

Johann Carlo: Actress who played Dixie on *Pee-wee's Playhouse* (1986–1987).

Kevin Carlson: Actor and puppeteer who voiced and operated Clocky, Floory, and Conky on *Pee-wee's Playhouse* (1987–1991).

Peggy Charren: Founder and president of Action for Children's Television.

Scott Chester: Personal assistant to Richard Abramson (1983–1987) and Paul Reubens (1987–1988) and associate producer of *Big Top Pee-wee*.

Doug Chiang: Animator for *Pee-wee's Playhouse* (1987–1991).

The Chiodo Brothers: Puppet builders for *The Pee-wee Herman Show* (2010–2011).

Jay Cotton: Composer of the score for both productions of *The Pee-wee Herman Show* and songwriter and coproducer of Pee-wee Herman's single, "I Know You Are, But What Am I?"

Valerie Curtin: Cowriter of *The Pee-wee Herman Story*, the film announced in 1999 that has yet to be released.

E.G. Daily: Actress who played Dottie in *Pee-wee's Big Adventure*.

Dave Daniels: Animator for *Pee-wee's Playhouse* and *Pee-wee's Playhouse Christmas Special*.

John DeFazio: Animator on *Pee-wee's Playhouse* (1986–1987).

Sal Denaro: Constructed the dinosaur family armatures for *Pee-wee's Playhouse* (1986–1987).

Doug Draizin: Paul Reubens' agent through Agency for the Performing Arts (1979–1983).

Danny Elfman: Composer for *Pee-wee's Big Adventure* and several episodes of *Pee-wee's Playhouse*.

Artie Esposito: Puppet builder and puppeteer for the Los Angeles run of *The Pee-wee Herman Show* (2010).

Prudence Fenton: Emmy Award–winning animation and effects producer for *Pee-wee's Playhouse* and cartoon and film consultant for *The Pee-wee Herman Show* (2010–2011).

Laurence (Larry) Fishburne: Actor who played Cowboy Curtis on *Pee-wee's Playhouse*.

Bill Freiberger: Animation director for *Pee-wee's Playhouse* (1989–1991).

Barbara Gallucci: Animator on *Pee-wee's Playhouse* (1986–1987).

Monica Ganas: Cowriter and actress who played Mrs. Jelly Donut in *The Pee-wee Herman Show* (1981).

Jesse Garcia: Actor who played Sergio in *The Pee-wee Herman Show* (2010).

Jared Geller: Associate producer of *The Pee-wee Herman Show* (2010–2011) who is also credited with convincing Paul Reubens to revive his stage show.

Richard "Golly" Goleszowski: Animator on *Pee-wee's Playhouse* (1986–1987).

Valeria Golino: Actress who played Gina in *Big Top Pee-wee*.

Sonny Grosso: Producer for *Pee-wee's Playhouse* (1989–1991).

Greg Harrison: Puppeteer and puppet builder on *Pee-wee's Playhouse* (1986–1987).

Phil Hartman: Actor who played Kap'n Karl in *The Pee-wee Herman Show* (1981) and Captain Carl in *Pee-wee's Playhouse* (1986–1987) and cowriter of *The Pee-wee Herman Show* (1981) and *Pee-wee's Big Adventure*.

Ric Heitzman: Emmy Award–winning art director who also voiced and operated puppets on *Pee-wee's Playhouse*.

Larry Jacobson: Producer for *Pee-wee's Playhouse* (1989–1991).

Vaughn Tyree Jelks: Actor who played Fabian on *Pee-wee's Playhouse* (1987–1988).

Haley Jenkins: Puppeteer for *The Pee-wee Herman Show* (2010–2011).

Lynette Johnson: Miniature clothing specialist who worked on *Pee-wee's Playhouse* (1987–1988).

Patrick Johnson: Puppet builder and puppeteer for the Los Angeles run of *The Pee-wee Herman Show* (2010).

Sean Johnson: Puppet builder and puppeteer for the Los Angeles run of *The Pee-wee Herman Show* (2010).

Stephen R. Johnson: Director of *Pee-wee's Playhouse* (1986–1987).

Victoria Johnson: Puppet designer and puppeteer for the Los Angeles run of *The Pee-wee Herman Show* (2010).

Phyllis Katz: Member of the Groundlings who taught the class in which Paul Reubens first developed the Pee-wee Herman character.

Dawna Kaufmann: Executive in charge of production of *The Pee-wee Herman Show* (1981).

Suzanne Kent: Actress who played Mrs. Rene on *Pee-wee's Playhouse* (1987–1991).

John Duke Kisch: Still photographer for *Pee-wee's Playhouse* (1986–1987).

Randal Kleiser: Director of *Big Top Pee-wee*.

Erik Kuska: Puppet builder and puppeteer for the Los Angeles run of *The Pee-wee Herman Show* (2010).

Kevin Ladson: A production assistant on *Pee-wee's Playhouse* (1986–1987).

Phil LaMarr: Actor who played Cowboy Curtis in *The Pee-wee Herman Show* (2010–2011).

Cyndi Lauper: Singer who provided the vocals for the *Pee-wee's Playhouse* theme song.

Glenn Lazzaro: Editor for the Magic Screen sequences for *Pee-wee's Playhouse* (1986–1987).

Joan Leizman: Actress who played Joan in *The Pee-wee Herman Show* (1981).

Gilbert Lewis: Actor who first played the King of Cartoons on *Pee-wee's Playhouse* (1986–1987).

Natasha Lyonne: Actress who played Opal on *Pee-wee's Playhouse* (1986–1987).

Karen Lyons: Toy designer for *Pee-wee's Playhouse* merchandise.

William Marshall: Actor who played the King of Cartoons on *Pee-wee's Playhouse* (1987–1991) after Gilbert Lewis.

Edie McClurg: Actress who played Hermit Hattie and cowrote *The Pee-wee Herman Show* (1981).

Bill McEuen: Paul Reubens' agent (1983–1986) and executive producer of *Pee-wee's Big Adventure*.

George McGrath: Cowriter for *Pee-wee's Playhouse* (1986–1988) and *Big Top Pee-wee*. Also a puppeteer who provided voices on *Pee-wee's Playhouse*.

Tom McLaughlin: Animator on *Pee-wee's Playhouse* (1987–1991).

Michael McLean: Paul Reubens' agent (circa 1991).

S. Epatha Merkerson: Actress who played Reba the Mail Lady on *Pee-wee's Playhouse*.

Josh Meyers: Actor who played Fireman Phineas in *The Pee-wee Herman Show* (2010–2011).

Penelope Ann Miller: Actress who portrayed Winnie in *Big Top Pee-wee*.

John Moody: Cowriter for *The Pee-wee Herman Show* (1981) and actor who played Mailman Mike in both productions of the show. He was also a writer on *Pee-wee's Playhouse* (1989–1991).

Alison Mork: Puppeteer who also provided voices on *Pee-wee's Playhouse*.

Mark Mothersbaugh: Composer of the *Pee-wee's Playhouse* theme song and for several episodes of the series.

Steve Oakes: Supervising producer for *Pee-wee's Playhouse* (1986–1987) and cofounder of the animation company Broadcast Arts.

Maceo Oliver: Understudy and provider of voices for the Los Angeles run of *The Pee-wee Herman Show* (2010).

Wayne Orr: Codirector of *Pee-wee's Playhouse* (1987–1989) and *Pee-wee's Playhouse Christmas Special.*

Gary Panter: Production designer and art director for *The Pee-wee Herman Show* (1981), Emmy Award–winning production designer for *Pee-wee's Playhouse*. He also cowrote a film with Paul Reubens entitled *Pee-wee's Big Adventure* that bears little resemblance to the 1985 film of the same title.

Nicole Panter: Actress who played Susan in *The Pee-wee Herman Show* (1981).

John Paragon: Actor who played Jambi the Genie in *Pee-wee's Playhouse* and both productions of *The Pee-wee Herman Show*. He also codirected *Pee-wee's Playhouse* (1989–1991) and voiced Pterri in *Pee-wee's Playhouse* (1986–1987, 1988–1991) and both productions of *The Pee-wee Herman Show*. He served as a cowriter on *Pee-wee's Playhouse* (1986–1987, 1988–1991), *Pee-wee's Playhouse Christmas Special* (1988), and *The Pee-wee Herman Show* (2010–2011).

Nick Park: Animator on *Pee-wee's Playhouse* (1986–1987).

Cassandra Peterson: Member of the Groundlings who served as an usherette for *The Pee-wee Herman Show* (1981).

Guy Pohlman: Stage crew and puppeteer for *The Pee-wee Herman Show* (1981).

Alisan Porter: Actress who played Lil' Punkin on *Pee-wee's Playhouse* (1987–1988).

Drew Powell: Actor who played the Bear in *The Pee-wee Herman Show* (2010–2011).

Dave Powers: Animation director on *Pee-wee's Playhouse* (1986–1987).

Judy Price: Vice president of children's programming at CBS throughout *Playhouse*'s run.

Max Robert: Cowriter on *Pee-wee's Playhouse* (1986–1988, 1989–1991).

Lance Roberts: Actor who played the King of Cartoons in *The Pee-wee Herman Show* (2010–2011).

Peter Rosenthal: Supervising producer for *Pee-wee's Playhouse* (1986–1987) and cofounder of Broadcast Arts.

Carla Rudy: Puppet builder and puppeteer for the Los Angeles run of *The Pee-wee Herman Show* (2010).

Jeff Sagansky: President of CBS Entertainment during run of *Pee-wee's Playhouse*.

Scott Sanders: Executive producer of *The Pee-wee Herman Show* (2010–2011).

Ken Sax: Still photographer for *Pee-wee's Playhouse* (1987–1989).

Brian Seff: Cowriter and actor who played Mr. Jelly Donut in *The Pee-wee Herman Show* (1981).

Ellen Shaw: One of Cyndi Lauper's backup singers inaccurately credited for singing the theme song to *Pee-wee's Playhouse*.

Steve Sleap: Puppet builder for *Pee-wee's Playhouse* (1987–1988).

Van Snowden: Puppeteer for *Pee-wee's Playhouse* (1987–1991).

Bill Steinkellner: Director of *The Pee-wee Herman Show* (1981) and cowriter for both productions of *The Pee-wee Herman Show*.

Lynne Marie Stewart: Actress who played Miss Yvonne in *Pee-wee's Playhouse* and both productions of *The Pee-wee Herman Show*.

Howard Stringer: President of CBS (1988–1995).

Shirley Stoler: Actress who played Mrs. Steve on *Pee-wee's Playhouse* (1986–1987).

Alex Timbers: Director of *The Pee-wee Herman Show* (2010–2011).

Phil Trumbo: Emmy Award–winning animation director for *Pee-wee's Playhouse* (1986–1987).

Basil Twist: Puppet consultant for the Los Angeles run of *The Pee-wee Herman Show* (2010) and puppet coordinator for the show's Broadway run (2010–2011).

Marc Tyler: Puppet builder for *Pee-wee's Playhouse* (1987–1988).

Michael Varhol: Cowriter of *Pee-wee's Big Adventure* and *Pee-wee's Playhouse* (1986–1987).

Michael Chase Walker: West Coast director of children's programming for CBS (c. 1985–1986).

Russ Walko: Puppet builder and puppeteer for the Los Angeles run of *The Pee-wee Herman Show* (2010).

Don Waller: Animator on *Pee-wee's Playhouse* (1987–1991).

Stephanie Walski: Actress who played Rapunzel on *Pee-wee's Playhouse* (1987–1988).

Shaun Weiss: Actor who played Elvis on *Pee-wee's Playhouse* (1986–1987).

Wayne White: Emmy Award–winning art director who also voiced and operated puppets on *Pee-wee's Playhouse*.

Diane Yang: Young actress who played Cher on *Pee-wee's Playhouse* (1986–1987).

Timothy Young: Toy designer for *Pee-wee's Playhouse* merchandise.

ACKNOWLEDGMENTS

THE "BIG ADVENTURE" Pee-wee Herman embarked on to reclaim his bicycle has nothing on the task of conceiving, writing, and preparing a book for release in less than two years. Although my name appears as the sole author of this book, there are many people whose efforts and assistance were instrumental to the successful completion of this project. The list that follows is by no means exhaustive, but provides a glimpse as to the size and scope of the team responsible for getting this project out of my imagination and into your hands.

First and foremost, I have to thank my editor Jen Hale and the team at ECW Press for entrusting a first-time author with a project of this magnitude. You've dealt with my never-ending lists of questions and given me the tools to be a better storyteller than I knew I could be. You gave me the opportunity to fulfill one of my life goals, an accomplishment that I am unspeakably proud of. For this you will always have my unending gratitude. I also owe thanks to Crissy Boylan, managing editor extraordinaire, the extremely talented Scott Barrie at Cyanotype for his awesome book cover and interior design, and ECW publishers Jack David and David Caron for their support and belief in this project.

My friend and mentor Chris Ryan, the godfather of this book, deserves a world of credit for encouraging me to forge ahead despite some early setbacks. I hope this makes you proud, and that it is a sizable apology for that story I wrote in seventh grade creative writing class that lives on in Hackensack High School infamy. Thank you for advising me against starting the first chapter of the book in a business meeting — which would have been incredibly boring — and for giving me the best piece of advice I received from anyone during this writing process: "Call Fiona."

I can say quite literally that this book wouldn't be in your hands right now if it weren't for the assistance of Fiona Sarne, one of my best friends who gave me a crash course in publishing and acted as my pro bono literary agent. Your advice was always right and, in every way possible, I owe this to you.

There aren't enough words to express how much Johanna Calle has been a guiding light through this process. You never complained about being a first-responder to my crises, bursts of enthusiasm, bouts with writer's block, and occasional audible laughs after I've typed something I thought was particularly clever. Your level of support has always been through the roof and I can't say enough how much I've enjoyed sharing this process with you. I love you and thank you for all you've done.

Terecille Basa-Ong, Josh Bellocchio, Angela De Gregorio, Rasha Jay, Caroline Krueger, Vanessa "Curly Fries" Matthews, Steven Pfeiffer, and Wendy Salkin have all been soundboards for ideas and gracious enough to provide me with feedback on drafts and the numerous cover designs. I couldn't imagine having gone through this process without your suggestions and support.

Although this project isn't an academic text in the conventional sense, I have relied heavily on my collegiate experiences from Rutgers University throughout this process. The tools I have gained in courses with Ann Fabian, Nicole Fleetwood, Susan Keith, Bruce Reynolds, Timothy Raphael, Erica Romaine, and Rob Snyder have been most helpful in researching, engaging with primary sources, conducting ethical and probing interviews, and writing purposefully.

While I appreciate the contributions of all subjects interviewed for this book, I am extremely grateful for the participation of Gary Austin, Steve Binder, Scott Chester, Dawna Kaufmann, George McGrath, John Duke Kisch, Steve Oakes, Judy Price, and Ken Sax. Your contributions to this project are ample and your assistance and friendship have been heartfelt. Thank you for your candor and for making yourselves available for "one more quick question." I've heard that writing a book is a lonely task, but you've certainly helped make the process more bearable.

I would be remiss if I didn't thank a number of Pee-wee fans I've met over the course of writing this book. People like Regina Burke, Brandon Hall, Christina Henriquez, Don Holcomb, Beau Kelley, Mitchell Klooster, Brittany Lynch, Dennis Manochio, Birgit Schuetz, Summer Violett, Ben Zurawski, and my pals on Facebook (www.facebook.com/caseengaines) were constant reminders of why this project matters. I thank all of you for your friendship and hope you enjoyed taking a look behind the scenes of one of your favorite television shows.

Most importantly, thanks go out to my parents for continuing to be behind me 110 percent. I can only imagine what goes through your minds half the time when I tell you what new project I'm tackling, but I credit you both with never making me feel like I'm biting off more than I can chew, even when I am. Thank you for encouraging me to live my dreams and loving me as always. I love you back.

NOTES

Ronald Reagan's quote that begins the Introduction is from Proclamation 5549, which was filed with the Office of the Federal Register on October 14, 1986. Peggy Charren's quote in the introduction is from Martin Booe's article, "Television Awareness Week Looks at Education, Commercialism — Toying with Children's Programming," from the October 11, 1986, edition of the *Daily News of Los Angeles*. The quote about *Pee-wee's Playhouse* being "utterly magical" is from Tom Shales' article, "The New Season — 'Law' Power NBC's Electrifying Look at Legal Life" from the September 15, 1986, edition of the *Washington Post*.

The chapter "From the Groundlings Up" was primarily inspired by conversations with Richard Abramson, Gary Austin, Scott Chester, Doug Draizin, Monica Ganas, Joan Leizman, Dawna Kaufmann, Nicole Panter, Guy Pohlman, and Brian Seff. Information on and Paul Reubens' quotes about his appearances on *The Gong Show* are from his November 29, 2004, NPR interview on *Fresh Air from WHHY*. Reubens' *Vanity Fair* quote is from Bruce Handy's article "Return from Planet Pee-wee" in the magazine's September 1999 issue, as is the reference to a "crazy, high-powered kid" from Reubens' youth. His quote about asking for a hard-boiled egg is from Mary Mozena's article "Comedy Central" in the October 2004 issue of *Los Angeles Magazine*, and is used with permission. Tommy Chong's quotes are from his book, *Cheech and Chong: The Unauthorized Autobiography*. Finally, the *Hollywood Reporter* article referenced toward the end of the chapter is from the article "Pee-wee Herman Tapes TV Pilot" in the February 6, 1981, issue.

The chapter "The Pitch and the Hit" was primarily inspired by conversations with Richard Abramson, Kent Burton, Johann Carlo, Scott Chester, Dave Daniels, Prudence Fenton, Kevin Ladson, Monica Ganas, Richard "Golly" Goleszowski, Dawna Kaufmann, Suzanne Kent, George McGrath, Steve Oakes, Nick Park, Guy Pohlman, Judy Price, Brian Seff, Phil

Trumbo, Michael Varhol, and Michael Chase Walker. The quotes and information about Gary Panter, Wayne White, and Ric Heitzman designing are from a videotape of the 14th Annual William S. Paley Television Festival honoring *Pee-wee's Playhouse* at the Museum of Television and Radio. The assertion that Paul Reubens made specific casting choices because he wanted diversity comes from his December 6, 2004, interview with Elvis Mitchell on KCRW's *The Treatment*. S. Epatha Merkerson's quote is from her June 11, 2008, interview with NPR.

"Puppetland, California" was primarily inspired by conversations with Richard Abramson, Steve Binder, Johann Carlo, Scott Chester, Doug Draizin, Prudence Fenton, Karen Lyons, George McGrath, Steve Oakes, Wayne Orr, Judy Price, Michael Varhol, and Stephanie Walski. All of Reubens quotes and some supplemental information in the merchandising section of this chapter are from Frank Thompson's article "Pee-wee Herman Talks Toys" from the December 1995 issue of *Collecting Toys* magazine. Reubens' quote about Pee-wee's active libido is from Marilyn Beck's article "Pee-wee Herman Discovers Sex" in the June 16, 1988, edition of the *Chicago Tribune*. The quote of the journalist expressing frustration at having to interview Reubens in character is from Bob Thomas's Associated Press article that was reprinted with the headline "Identifying Paul Reubens Can Be an Adventure" in the August 21, 1988, edition of the *Beaver Country Times*.

"A Christmas Story" was inspired by conversations with Steve Binder, Prudence Fenton, Joel Fletcher, George McGrath, Wayne Orr, and Judy Price. Unless otherwise cited, quotes from Alison Mork, John Paragon, Lynne Stewart, and Paul Reubens are from the audio commentary track on the *Pee-wee's Playhouse Christmas Special* 2004 DVD release from Image Entertainment. The *Newsday* article referred to at the beginning of the chapter is from Joanne Ostrow's article "An Offbeat Comic Is Saturday's Hero to the Kidvid Set" in the November 29, 1986, issue. Reubens' quote about adults feeling "semi-groggy" and getting "a lot of cool new stuff," along with Dinah Shore and Annette Funicello's quotes, are from John Milward's article "A Pee-wee Christmas Playhouse" from the December 20, 1988, issue of *Newsday*. Reubens' quote about the special being "thin on plot" is from Lynn Hoogenboom's article "Mecka-lecka-hi, Mecka-hiney-ho [sic], Now it's Time for Pee-wee's Show" from the December 18, 1988, issue of the *St. Petersburg Times*. Although most of Steve Binder's quotes come from new interviews, his words about "hardcore *Playhouse* fans" comes from Matt Roush's *USA Today* article "Pee-wee's Merry Kitsch-Mas," which ran on December 21, 1988.

The chapter "Foreclosure" comes primarily from conversations with George McGrath and Judy Price. The *Newsday* article cited early on in the chapter is Jane Wollman's article "The Real Pee-wee" from December 17, 1989, as is Reubens' quote about directing, writing, and producing. Lynne Stewart's quote, along with Reubens' quotes later in the chapter about learning Spanish and the perception that CBS canceled *Pee-wee's Playhouse*, is from Brian M. Raftery's article "Pee-wee Turns 20" that ran in the September 1, 2006, edition of *Entertainment Weekly*. Michael McLean's quote comes from Steve Daly's article "Gracias, Pee-wee Herman" from the same magazine's May 3, 1991, issue. Allee Willis's quote is from Peter Wilkinson's *Rolling Stone* article "Who Killed Pee-wee Herman?" that ran on September 22, 1991. The details of Reubens' sentencing are from Larry Rohter's article "Pee-wee Herman Enters a Plea of No Contest" in the November 8, 1991, issue of *Time*.

"P2K" was primarily inspired by conversations with Kent Burton, Prudence Fenton, Monica Ganas, Sean Johnson, Dawna Kaufmann, Suzanne Kent, Erik Kusha, George McGrath, Carla Rudy, and Brian Seff. Reubens' quote about "not shooting up" is from Joel Stein's article "Bigger than Pee-wee" from the April 1, 2001, edition of *Time*. Reubens' description of *The Pee-wee Herman Story*'s plot and it being cowritten with Valerie Curtin is from a videotape of the Museum of Television and Radio's seminar series celebrating the 25th anniversary of the Groundlings from September 29, 1999. The *Esquire* quote about Reubens' performance in *Blow* is from their April 1, 2005, article "The Blow by Blow." Reubens' quotes about the plot of the *Playhouse* film are from his January 17, 2010, Q&A session after *The Pee-wee Herman Show* at Club Nokia, as reported by George "El Guapo" Roush for LatinoReview.com. Reubens' quote about Taylor Lautner is from his December 9, 2009, interview with *Access Hollywood*. His quote about "riding a bike" is from David Ng's article "Pee-wee Herman Ready for His Stage Comeback" from the August 10, 2009, edition of the *Los Angeles Times*, while his quote about Gellar calling him is from the December 11, 2009, Associated Press article "Pee-wee Herman's Big Comeback." Scott Sanders' quote is from David Ng's article "Fans of Pee-wee Herman Angry over Show's Postponement" from the October 7, 2009, *Los Angeles Times*. Reubens' quotes from *Dateline* are from his interview with Stone Phillips that aired on April 5, 2004. The information about Chris Rock is from the aforementioned Club Nokia Q&A, and the references to S. Epatha Merkerson and Lawrence Fishburne are from Raferty's *Entertainment Weekly* article cited for the previous chapter.

All of the information from the chapter "Appraising the Playhouse" is from conversations with Gary Austin, Steve Binder, Kent Burton, Johann Carlo, Kevin Carlson, Scott Chester, Dave Daniels, Prudence Fenton, Monica Ganas, Troy Hughes-Palmer, Vaughn Tyree Jelks, Steve Johnson, Victoria Johnson, Dawna Kaufmann, Suzanne Kent, John Duke Kisch, Glenn Lazzaro, George McGrath, Steve Oakes, Wayne Orr, Judy Price, Ken Sax, Phil Trumbo, Marc Tyler, Michael Chase Walker, and Stephanie Walski.

INDEX

Aardman Studios, 53, 54

Abramson, Richard, 30–34, 38, 47, 56–57, 71–75, 94, 99, 102, 209

Action for Children's Television, 2

Agency of Performing Arts (APA), 12–13, 25, 27–30

Alan, Lori, 133, 135, 141

Alex in Wonderland (puppet company), 133

Apatow, Judd, 140

Avalon, Frankie, 108, 112

Bartlett, Craig, 87–88

Bear (character), 132

Big Top Pee-wee, 71, 91, 93–100, 101, 103, 105, 112, 113, 125, 144, 148, 165

Billy Baloney (character), 77, 78, 91

Binder, Steve, 83–87, 101–103, 107–109, 111, 114, 116, 146–147

Blow, 128

Bowie, David, 110

Broadcast Arts, 36–40, 42–43, 48, 53–54, 60–61, 71–76, 83, 87

Burton, Kent, 54–55, 62–63, 88, 141, 147

Burton, Tim, 31–33, 36, 94

Bush, Kelly, 129–130

Captain Carl (character), 56–57 *see also* Kap'n Karl

Captain Kangaroo, 7

Carlo, Johann, 57–58, 82, 147

Carlson, Kevin, 78–79, 83, 109, 141, 147

Cartoon Network, 3, 114, 146

CBS, 1, 14 35–36, 38, 42–44, 64, 65–66, 71, 73, 75, 99, 101–102, 114, 116, 121, 123, 129, 151

Chairry (character), 52–53, 89, 91, 111, 127, 133–134

Charo, 108 110, 112

Charren, Peggy, 2

Cheech and Chong's Next Movie, 12

Cher (character), *see* Yang, Diane

Cher (singer), 108, 109–110

Chester, Scott, 47, 95, 99, 148

Chiang, Doug, 88

Chicky Baby (character), 51, 52, 111, 137

Chiodo Brothers, The, 133, 134

Chong, Tommy, 12–13, 80

Clocky (character), 16, 78–79, 90, 135

Conky 2000 (character), 50, 83, 90, 109, 127, 133, 135

Cool Cat (character), 51, 52, 111

Cotton, Jay, 18–19, 40

Cowboy Curtis (character), 58, 107, 127, 130, 132, 135, 140, 142, 143

Cowntess (character), 76–77, 109,

Cuomo, Jimmy, 105, 106

Curtin, Valerie, 126

Daily, E.G., 96

Daniels, Dave, 54–55, 62–63, 88, 148

DeFazio, John, 62

Del Rubio Triplets, The, 108, 110–111

Denaro, Sal, 55

Depp, Johnny, 127

Dinosaur Family (characters), 37, 43, 54, 55, 88, 106, 141, 147

Dirty Dog (character), 51, 52, 111

Dixie the Cab Driver (character), 58, 81, 147

Dr. Mondo (character), 23

Draizin, Doug, 12–13, 15, 27, 29, 70

Duvall, Shelley, 31

Elfman, Danny, 164, 210

El Chunky Boobabi (character), 127, 140

El Hombre (character), 117–118

Elvis (character), 191, 213

Emmy Awards, 65, 93, 105, 118, 125

Esposito, Artie, 133–134, 136

Fabian (character), 149

Face in the Crowd, A, 126–127

Fenton, Prudence, 5, 48, 60–62, 65, 78, 87, 94, 104, 105, 106, 127, 148

Fireman Phineas (character), 132, 143
Fishburne, Laurence (Larry), 58, 119, 132, 140
Fletcher, Joel, 104–105
Floory (character), 78, 79, 90
Flores, Mario "Ivan," 18
Francis Buxton (character), 32
Freiberger, Bill, 117–118
Fridell, Lexy, 141
Funicello, Annette, 108, 112, 124

Gabor, Zsa Zsa, 108–109
Gallucci, Barbara, 62
Ganas, Monica, 18, 26, 62, 67, 139, 148
    see also Rick and Ruby
Garcia, Jesse, 132
Geller, Jared, 129, 130
Ginger (character), 135
Globey (character), 76, 135
Goldberg, Whoopi, 108, 112–113, 141
Goleszowski, Richard "Golly," 53–54, 55
Golino, Valeria, 94–95, 96
Gong Show, The, 9
Grosso, Sonny, 116
Groundlings, The, 8–9, 12, 15–18, 19, 21, 22, 57, 58, 80, 81, 132, 146
Groundling Theatre, The, 7–8, 11, 12, 13, 18, 21–22, 23, 27, 42–43, 58, 130, 138, 139

Hammy (character), 23
Haris, Niki, 107
Harrison, Greg, 49, 50, 74, 83
Hartman, Phil, 15–16, 19, 20, 30, 56–57, 70, 130
HBO, 2, 25–26, 40, 41, 48, 207
Henson, Lisa, 31
Hermit Hattie (character), 7, 20
Heitzman, Ric, 48, 51, 52, 53, 76, 105, 106, 130
Hilarious Betty and Eddie, The (characters), 9, 11

Howdy Doody, 7, 5

"I Know You Are, But What Am I?"(phrase), 3, 10, 97
"I Know You Are, But What Am I?"(song), 40
ID Public Relations, 129

Jacobson, Larry, 116
Jambi the Genie (character), 3, 7, 16, 48, 82, 132, 142, 143, 152
Jelks, Vaughn Tyree, 82, 149
Jenkins, Haley, 135, 141
Joe Longtoe (character), 11
Johnson, Lynette, 78
Johnson, Magic, 108, 109
Johnson, Patrick, 133, 136, 137
Johnson, Sean, 133, 134, 137, 138, 141
Johnson, Stephen R., 55, 84, 85
Johnson, Victoria, 134–135
Jones, Grace, 108, 109, 110–111
Just Jeff (character), 9–10

Kap'n Karl (character), 7, 15–16, 23, 49, 56, 130
    see also Captain Carl
Katz, Phyllis, 8, 9
Kaufmann, Dawna, 14–16, 18–22, 24–29, 66, 126, 139, 149
Kent, Suzanne, 58–59, 80–81, 99, 140–141, 149
King of Cartoons, The (character), 58, 81, 113, 127, 132–133, 143
Kisch, John Duke, 150
Klein, Marty, 29, 30
Kleiser, Randal, 94
Kristofferson, Kris, 98
Kuska, Erik, 138, 139

Ladson, Kevin, 58, 59
LaMarr, Phil, 5, 132
lang, k.d., 108, 110, 111
Late Night with David Letterman, 29, 30, 36, 40, 102,

Late Night with Jimmy Fallon, 141
Lauper, Cyndi, 63, 64–65, 124
Lazzaro, Glenn, 45–46, 150
Leizman, Joan, 17, 22–23, 80, 130
Lewis, Gilbert, 13, 58, 81, 133
Lil' Punkin (character), see Alisan Porter
Little Richard, 108, 110
Louthan, Guy, 86
Lyonne, Natasha, 82
Lyons, Karen, 89

Madalena-Lloyd, Deborah, 105
Magic Screen (character), 43–45, 88, 90, 109, 110, 127, 134–135
Mailman Mike (character), 7, 16, 57, 130, 132, 143
Marshall, William, 81, 113, 133
Martin, Steve, 13, 21, 24, 30, 41
Matchbox Toys, 89–91
McClurg, Edie, 16, 19, 20, 78
McEuen, Bill, 30, 31, 34, 36, 38
McGinnis, Charlotte, 9
McGrath, George, 42–43, 45, 50, 51, 57, 59, 63–64, 69, 71,76, 77, 80, 83, 91, 93, 94, 95–96, 98, 99–100, 109, 110, 111, 117, 121, 130, 131, 132, 141, 146
McLaughlin, Tom, 88
McLean, Michael, 118
Merkerson, S. Epatha, 57–58, 119, 140
Meyers, Josh, 132
Michaels, Lorne, 56
Miller, Penelope Ann, 96, 98
Miss Yvonne (character), 5, 7, 16, 23, 47, 92, 102, 105–106, 132, 142, 147
Monsieur LeCroq (character), 16
Moody, John, 16, 57, 130, 132
Mork, Alison, 44, 51, 52–53, 111, 112, 117, 130, 132, 133 141
Mothersbaugh, Mark, 50, 61, 64
Mrs. Jelly Donut (character), 7, 18, 67, 139, 148

Mrs. Rene (character), 80–81, 140, 149
   see also Rita Chandelier; Sidney the Agent
Mrs. Steve (character), 58, 80
Mr. Jelly Donut (character), 7, 18, 41, 132
Mr. Kite (character), 51
Mr. Knucklehead (character), 49
Mr. Window (character), 51, 135
MTV, 36, 38, 40, 48, 55, 73, 114

Newman, Tracy, 12

Oakes, Steve, 36, 40, 42, 53, 60, 65, 73, 74, 75, 145, 150
Oliver, Maceo, 133
Opal (character), see Lyonne, Natasha
Orr, Wayne, 86, 87, 93, 106–107, 109, 110–111, 112, 113, 150–151

Panter, Gary, 18, 19, 29, 48, 53, 70, 76, 105, 127
Panter, Nicole, 18, 19, 22, 23, 24–25, 27, 28
Paragon, John, 5, 11, 16, 24, 29, 42, 49, 56, 69, 71, 82, 90, 101, 103, 107, 108, 109, 110, 112, 116, 130, 131, 132, 152
Park, Nick, 53
Paul, J. Reid, 63
Penny (character), 53, 54, 87, 91–92, 106
Peterson, Cassandra, 15, 17, 29
Pee-wee Herman (character)
   creation of, 10
   exhaustion with, 115–118
   merchandise of, 89–92, 101, 123, 142, 144
   Spike TV Guys' Choice Awards appearance of, 129
Pee-wee Herman Party, The, 30–31, 34
Pee-wee Herman Show, The (1981), 2,
7, 15–29, 40, 42, 49, 56, 57, 58, 66, 67, 126, 127, 130, 143, 148, 149, 152
   at the Groundling Theatre, 21–25
   at the Roxy Theatre, 22, 25–26
   creation of, 15–20
   first performances of, 21
   HBO On Location taping of, 25–26
   problems with, 22–29
Pee-wee Herman Show, The (2010–2011), 128–145
   at Club Nokia, 138, 139, 140
   at the Music Box, 130, 131
   at the Stephen Sondheim Theatre, 141, 142–143
   creation of, 128–129, 133–138
   criticism of, 131
   first staged reading of, 130
   first performance of, 138–139
   success of, 140
Pee-wee Herman Story, The, 125–126
Pee-wee's Big Adventure, 2, 31–34, 36–37, 41, 42, 56, 66, 69–70, 95–96, 98, 102, 125, 127, 132, 133, 140, 141, 144
Pee-wee's Playhouse: The Movie, 126–127, 132, 140–141
Pee-wee's Playhouse Christmas Special, 101–114, 115, 116, 141, 146, 150
   "Jingle Bell Rock," 111
   "Little Drummer Boy, The," 110
   "Oh It's Christmas in the Playhouse," 107–108
   "Twelve Days of Christmas, The," 111
   "Winter Wonderland," 111
Philbin, Regis, 21, 142
Pinky Lee Show, The, 15
Playhouse Gang (characters), 82, 149, 152
Pohlman, Guy, 19, 21–22, 26, 27, 28, 67
Porter, Alisan, 82

Powell, Drew, 132
Powers, Dave, 50
Price, Judy, 36, 41, 42, 44, 47, 65, 66, 71–72, 73, 75, 84, 89, 92, 99–100, 114, 115–116, 118, 121–123, 145, 151
Pterry-Dactyl (Pterri, character), 16–17, 49, 71, 78, 82, 89, 90, 91, 135, 136
Puppetland, 7, 16, 42, 51, 69–100, 102, 107, 127
Puppetland Band, 111, 136–137

Rapunzel (character), 152
Randy (character), 52, 77, 78, 133
Raum, Jeff, 63
Reba the Mail Lady (character), 57, 140
Ricardo (character), 81
Rick and Ruby (characters), 18
   see also Ganas, Monica; Seff, Brian
Rita Chandelier (character), 80–81
Rivers, Joan, 108, 109, 124
Robert, Max, 42, 80, 105
Roberts, Lance, 132
Rock, Chris, 140
Rodriguez, Roland, 81
Romani, Dora, 18
Rosenthal, Peter, 36, 42
Roxy Theatre, The, 22, 25, 130
Rubenfeld, Abby, 7
Rubenfeld, Luke, 7
Rubenfeld, Judy, 15
Rubenfeld, Milton, 15
Rubenfeld, Paul, 6, 7
Rudy, Carla, 136, 138–139
Rust, Paul, 140

Sagansky, Jeff, 122
Salvador Sanchez (character), 18
Sanders, Scott, 130–131
Saturday Night Live (SNL), 13, 14, 28, 56

Sax, Ken, 151
Seff, Brian, 18, 41, 132
    see also Rick and Ruby
Sergio the Repairman (character), 131–132, 143
Sham Wow (character), 135–136, 137
    Ghost of, 136
Shapiro, Robert, 30
Shaw, Ellen, 64–65
Shore, Dinah, 108, 110–111
Sidney the Agent (character), 80
Singleton, John, 119
Sleap, Steve, 76–78
Snowden, Van, 77
Soupy Sales, The, 14, 15
Steinkellner, Bill, 131
Stewart, Lynne Marie, 5, 16, 17, 22, 23, 24, 29, 47, 56, 99, 102, 105–106, 118, 130, 132
Stringer, Howard, 122

Stoler, Shirley, 59, 80
Susan (character), 23
Swazzle (puppet company), 133–138, 141

Timbers, Alex, 130–131, 134
Larriva, Tito, 23
Tito the Lifeguard (character), 81
Tonight Show with Jay Leno, The, 125, 141–142
Trevino, Vic, 81
Trumbo, Phil, 145, 151
Turturice, Robert, 105
Twilight Theatre, 41
Twist, Basil, 135
Tyler, Marc, 76, 77, 78

Vance the Talking Pig (character), 91
Varhol, Michael, 30, 42, 43, 69–70, 71

Walker, Michael Chase, 35, 36, 37, 38, 41, 42, 65–66, 73, 151–152
Walko, Russ, 213
Waller, Don, 88
Walski, Stephanie, 82, 152
Warner Brothers, 30, 31, 33, 34
Weintraub, Jerry, 70
Weiss, Shaun, 82
White, Wayne, 48–49, 51, 52, 53, 76, 77–78, 105, 106, 135
Willis, Allee, 119–120
Winfrey, Oprah, 108, 109
Winky Dink and You, 43–44
Writers Guild of America strike (1988), 101–103
Winnie (character), 96

Yang, Diane, 82
Young, Timothy, 90–92